Jakarta Jive

A story of survival
in a city of upheaval

Jakarta Jive

A story of survival
in a city of upheaval

Jeremy Allan

PT. Metafor Intermedia Indonesia
Jl. Cempaka Putih Barat III no. 29A
Jakarta 10520, Indonesia
e-mail: info@metaforpublishing.com
http://www.metaforpublishing.com
Ph. +62-21-42800516 Fax. +62-21-42800515

Story editor : Jamie James

Book design by Muhammad Roniyadi
Photographs of Jeremy Allan © October 2001 by Sinartus Sosrodjojo/Jiwa Foto.
All rights reserved.

10 09 08 07 06 05 04 03 02 01   10 9 8 7 6 5 4 3 2 1

National Library of Indonesia Cataloguing-in-Publication Data

Allan, Jeremy
    Jakarta Jive / Jeremy Allan. - Jakarta :
Metafor Publishing, 2001.
viii , 227 pages ; 21.5 cm

ISBN 979-3019-05-0

1. Jakarta - Deskripsi.   I. Judul.

                                                     915.983

To Daniel

Contents

Jakarta Jive

Prologue

Chicken Market Bridge

NOTHING I HAD WITNESSED DURING TWO DECADES of living in Indonesia matched the spectacle of shirtless men shuffling in total silence across the Chicken Market Bridge, an eighteenth-century span across a canal in the heart of Jakarta's colonial-era district. Against a backdrop of two-hundred-year-old buildings, the men could have been coolies hauling wares to a Europe-bound schooner anchored at the nearby harbor. However, instead of bags of coffee or sugar, the men carried modern consumer goods like electric fans, televisions, or readily saleable products such as computers, fax machines, and office chairs. One slightly built man, bent almost double under the weight of a refrigerator, could have stepped from a historical lithograph depicting wiry, immensely strong laborers dwarfed by the loads they carried.

The "coolies" were actually looters caught in the act during the city-wide riots of 14 May 1998, stripped of their shirts for easy identification should they attempt to escape custody and carrying the evidence of their wrongdoing as police marched them into detention.

Unimaginative guidebook writers and hack journalists often describe Indonesia as "a nation sitting atop a volcano," alluding to the pent-up social pressures which had been threatening to erupt for decades. That day, overworked metaphor became appalling reality as the legendary Indonesian patience and tolerance gave way to unrestrained savagery in the wake of a region-wide crisis which seemed to have erased years of economic progress overnight.

Thousands of local youths, together with rural residents bused in for the occasion by unknown agents, had looted and burned homes and businesses throughout Jakarta. Ethnic-Chinese Indonesians were the hardest hit, suffering both loss of livelihood and, in dozens of documented cases, the terror of systematic rape. In some areas, rioters themselves became victims. Authorities estimate that more than a thousand looters perished in the collapse of burning buildings, apparently seized by a desire to grab as much as possible, heedless of personal safety.

Seen from the air, with debris-strewn streets and whole districts under a pall of smoke from burning buildings and vehicles, I imagined Jakarta would resemble a city devastated by natural forces. But on the ground, I felt I had wandered into nothing more serious than an excessively rowdy block party. As I walked through one major riot area, I saw no signs of human suffering, nor did I feel any sort of menace from the hundreds of rioters on the streets. I was either ignored or the object of enthusiastic greetings, no different from my customary reception when strolling in Jakarta on a normal day.

That evening my e-mail inbox was full of frantic enquiries about my safety from family and friends at home, in Canada. I assured everyone I was fine, then received another flurry of requests to explain what was happening. One message was from a college classmate in my home town of Vancouver, who wanted to interview me by telephone for the morning radio show he produced. Because of the time difference, the interview took place in the late evening, when I was exhausted from a full day of driving around the city, surveying the damage. As I tried to put this multi-faceted event into a few sound bites, I felt my interviewer was becoming annoyed at my seemingly self-contradictory statements. I do not remember exactly what I said during the interview, but I suppose I sounded somewhat like an exasperating Zen master who answers mutually exclusive multiple-choice questions with a single word: "Yes." That, for example, would have been my answer if the interviewer had asked whether President Soeharto was a cold-blooded dictator who plundered the nation, or a benevolent leader who created a better life for his people.

While Soeharto's rule fostered widespread corruption and human rights abuses, he was also responsible for three decades of steady economic growth and improvement of public welfare, which, the crisis notwithstanding, had brought his nation to within shouting distance of self-sustaining industrial development.

How about the Indonesians themselves? the interviewer might ask. Are they a race of brutal savages, or are they among the gentlest, most hospitable people on earth? Again, I would answer yes. Besides the slaughter in the riots of May 1998, Jakarta would see other senseless massacres throughout the year. But even the foreign journalists hunting sensational stories of unrestrained butchery were impressed by Indonesian generosity and kindness.

My ambivalent relationship with Indonesia began in the late seventies, when a geophysical exploration company desperate for manpower during those oil-boom years snatched me from a backpacker's dormitory in Singapore. Twenty-four hours later, I found myself in the Kalimantan rainforest, riding herd on several hundred local workers contracted to an international seismic-survey crew. My only qualification for the job was the ability—essential for serious budget travelers—to adjust to isolation and strange environments, which I put to good use during my two-year career in the oil industry.

When I was laid off after the end of the oil boom, I spent several months exploring remote regions of the archipelago before settling in Jakarta, intending to live off my savings while forging a writing career. I adjusted well to my new life as a down-market resident foreigner—perhaps a little too well. When a group of young men living in one household started committing acts of petty theft around the neighborhood, my neighbors and I held an impromptu meeting to discuss the problem. One offered to ask his brother, an army officer, for assistance in contacting an elite army squad which, at the time, was assassinating known criminals in an effort to curb the growing crime rate. Along with my neighbors, I nodded my assent to the proposal, giving my tacit approval to a summary execution.

This was my first real awareness of life in Soeharto's Indonesia. The year I moved to Jakarta, 1982, was halfway into the thirty-year term of his New

Order government, until now the most successful attempt to transform this multi-lingual, multi-cultural, multi-just-about-everything archipelago into a unified nation. Since declaring independence from the Dutch in 1945, the republic had suffered through years of guerilla warfare, embarked on a brave attempt at instituting a system of western-style parliamentary democracy, and experienced economic chaos, as the charismatic President Soekarno substituted rousing rhetoric for effective government. Along the way, the Indonesian people suffered a mass slaughter seldom equaled in modern times, and finally arrived at a workable system of government which delivered stability and relative prosperity—and all the civil rights of an anthill.

A business-friendly government, social stability, and improving standards of public health and education made Indonesia an attractive place to invest from the late eighties onward. Glass-walled office towers, flashy shopping malls, and sprawling industrial parks attested to the public and private-sector money pouring into the country. I rode the economic boom, enjoying moderate success as a travel journalist, then as an advertising copywriter. My backpacking days over, I married an Indonesian woman and settled into a middle-class Indonesian lifestyle.

Like most of my neighbors, I spared little thought to the nation our children would someday inherit. Though we were fully aware of the rampant corruption and inefficiency at all levels of society, such concerns were swept under the luxurious carpet of six percent annual economic growth. In the early nineties, the deregulation of the financial sector allowed me a glimpse under that rug, when local companies hired me to produce English-language printed and video material for presentations to potential foreign investors. During the course of researching these projects, and through discussions with business journalists and academics, I gained some insight into the workings of the economy. I came to share the opinion of many astute observers that disaster was around the corner. Although to my knowledge no one foresaw the magnitude of the eventual collapse, we believed that the growing foreign debt, over-reliance on imports, and inflated costs resulting from widespread corruption would bring the party to a premature end.

When the hammer finally fell, Jakarta was transformed. The free-falling exchange rate of the Indonesian rupiah against major currencies stopped the import-dependent economy in its tracks. Jagged beams and girders rising from mud-filled lots were all that remained of construction projects abandoned in mid-stream. Fewer cars were on the streets, and beggars were more numerous, their eyes filled with desperation and fear. Some referred to the months after the fall of Soeharto as a *jaman edan*, a poetic term for a chaotic time when evil is rewarded and good punished. But the complex nature of the period defeats any attempts at generalization. For example, the plunging rupiah brought fortune as well as disaster. Local news photographers, formerly among the poorest of my acquaintances, bought new camera equipment and motorcycles as foreign publications paid in hard currency for shots of Indonesian misery and social unrest.

Indonesia's only previous change in leadership was also a *jaman edan*, when Soeharto maneuvered

Soekarno out of power during an eighteen-month period in the mid-sixties during which half a million Indonesians died in anti-Communist pogroms. Then, as in 1998, an objective, reliable account of events did not—and most likely will never—exist. If the big picture is sketchy, some details are crystal clear. A *jaman edan*, while a period of turmoil, is also a time of transformation. For some—the rape victims, the families of slain students—that year brought only trauma and grief. But for many others, 1998 was a year of hope and renewal, a time of successful struggles to find a foothold in a new world. This chronicle of the *jaman edan* will be told by looking through the eyes of those who lived through it—beginning with Monica, an ethnic Chinese economics student at Trisakti University, holed up in the library while many of her classmates were in the campus parking lot, trying to bring down a government.

Sea of Fire

EXUBERANT SHOUTS FROM THE PARKING LOT distracted Monica as she pored over her dismal textbook in the Trisakti University Economics Faculty building. Through a nearby window she had an elevated view of the parking lot on the northwest corner of the campus and the adjacent major intersection of two six-lane thoroughfares, with a four-lane expressway arching overhead. The window normally afforded a vista of students chatting in groups or milling around, and, on the streets beyond, the near-permanent traffic jam, graphic proof of both Indonesia's flourishing economy and intractable infrastructure problems.

On this afternoon, a large percentage of the Trisakti student body was massed at the campus perimeter, facing a phalanx of soldiers and policemen in riot helmets and shields. Unknown to the demonstrators and rank-and-file troops on the street, military snipers were concealed on the expressway fly-over. The event was one of the largest and most enthusiastic student demonstrations calling for President Soeharto's resignation and an all-out attack against the high-level corruption and mismanagement that had helped turn a robust, industrializing nation into an economic basket case.

Trisakti, a name that would become a rallying cry for the movement to force a long-overdue change in national leadership, is an unlikely catalyst of social revolution. This modern campus in a lively central commercial district is the breeding ground for the second generation of Indonesia's emergent middle class: "Indoyups." During the previous weeks of student demonstrations, these Indoyups-in-training were distinguished only by their absence, to no one's surprise. Few believed these spoiled kids would ever take to the streets, unless it was to protest the chronic lack of parking space around the campus.

The week before the current demonstration, Forkot, one of the more radical inter-school organizations coordinating the city-wide protests, had lost patience with Trisakti's perceived lack of support for the student movement. In a mock awards ceremony, a Forkot member presented Trisakti's predominantly male student activist committee with a set of women's underwear, a pointed—and somewhat sexist—rebuke for their less-than-conscientious approach to social revolution.

Trisakti's embryonic Indoyups actually had little to fear. In contrast to other occasions in the Republic of Indonesia's history, when students protesting real or imagined governmental malfeasance were rapidly and violently suppressed, the students of May 1998, like those of the sixties, seemed to enjoy the tacit approval and support of the military.

While the police and army troops stood by, the students could say, and do, anything they wished, as long they remained within campus boundaries. Both sides lined up neatly along those arbitrary demarcation lines, students shouting reasonable, even polite and respectful slogans, such as "Mr. Soeharto, please step down." The young soldiers good-naturedly belted out patriotic songs in reply. The atmosphere resembled a friendly verbal sparring contest—a favorite pastime among Indonesian village youth—rather than a tense confrontation between a defiant populace and the forces of state oppression.

Emboldened by the groundswell of public opinion and by expressions of sympathy and support given by front-line soldiers to foreign and domestic reporters, the Trisakti demonstrators planned to redeem their honor as stalwart revolutionaries by bursting forth from the campus and marching a kilometer down the adjoining expressway to the heavily guarded complex housing the MPR, Indonesia's version of—or sorry excuse for—a representative assembly, which had recently reelected Soeharto for a seventh five-year term.

While the crowd of demonstrators prepared for their historic march, Monica was facing increasing difficulty concentrating on the arcane economic concepts she had to understand, or at least parrot, to pass her upcoming exams. Deciding she needed a break, she walked out of the front entrance and into the periphery of the crowd. As she listened to the excited chatter of students and heard the shouts and songs from the front-line demonstrators, Monica felt her resolve fade away. Like most young urban Indonesian women, Monica's demure manner hides a party girl waiting to bust loose. The gathering seemed as festive as a day at the amusement park. Initial mission forgotten, Monica drifted into the crowd.

Monica's flawless pale skin, long, silky hair and fine features attract attention in any crowd. She received more than her share of sidelong glances as she made her way toward the main body of the demonstration. Indonesians of Chinese ancestry like

Monica tend to avoid large assemblies of *pribumi*, as Indonesians of Malay ancestry call themselves. Like a spy or a fugitive, when Monica found herself in such a situation she always had an escape route planned, just in case. But today, Monica let herself be engulfed by the throng. After all, these students were from her own class: affluent, educated, from good families, supposedly in control of the primal passions that, in seconds, can transform a cheerful crowd into a rampaging mob. Monica felt little anxiety as she drifted through the mass of students, occasionally greeting an acquaintance as she enjoyed the boisterous chanting and genial catcalls directed at the troops.

Monica was a short distance from the campus perimeter when the students burst from their self-imposed confines and surged forward into the street. Instead of confronting the police directly, who were stunned by the sudden change in events, they turned toward the expressway leading to the MPR. They did not get far. Monica was caught in a dense mass of humanity as the vanguard was stopped in their tracks by a line of troops. Students in the front ranks sat down in defiance, those behind milled aimlessly or, as Monica did, returned to the campus.

At five p.m., an officer spoke into a bullhorn, requesting the remaining students, many of them continuing their sit-down protest in front of the riot troops, to return to the campus. After a brief deliberation among the student coordinators, the sitting students rose and retreated behind the campus perimeter.

Monica watched the students return, oblivious to the staccato cracks, like distant fireworks, coming from the flyover. As students started running, Monica heard terrified shouts and screams. When I talked to her about it months afterward, I could see the fear in her eyes still.

"I wished, more than anything, I had stayed in the library," Monica told me. "It was horrible. When I heard the screams as the military started shooting, I ran behind a building and cried. I didn't know what would happen if I tried to go home, so I just wandered around the campus, like in a daze, not knowing where to go."

Later, when the shock of events wore off, Monica realized that her parents must have heard about the shootings. As the nearest public telephones were on the other side of the campus, a hard struggle through the dense crowd, Monica looked around for a cell phone she could borrow to call and reassure her family. She noticed a group of students clustered around a concrete barrier post on the campus perimeter, several speaking softly into cell phones. As Monica approached, she could see an object resembling a large, blood-soaked sponge placed on a concrete rail post. Only when she overheard others describing how a student's skull was cleaved by a bullet and the brain cleanly detached did she realize she was viewing a grisly rebuke to the soldiers for their violence against Indonesia's future intellectual elite.

The students were finally allowed to leave the campus in early evening. Monica returned home to find her parents understandably near hysteria. Monica gave them a heavily edited version of the day's events, letting them believe she had been trapped in the library, not in the midst of a crowd under fire from military sharpshooters.

Nina, a pribumi friend and classmate, telephoned Monica the next morning with news of a giant rally to honor the fallen students. Her parents objected strenuously to Monica's leaving the house. Though she had not known any of the victims, she felt that it would be somehow disloyal to remain at home while her classmates demonstrated their grief and anger.

After another phone call from Nina, Monica sought support from her grandmother, who was staying with the family after anti-Chinese riots had destroyed their dry-goods shop in Malang two months before. The old lady just shrugged her shoulders and offered sound, practical advice. "Do what you want," she said, "just don't get shot."

At the Trisakti campus Monica listened to reformist politicians praise the fallen students. The four were proclaimed Pahlawan Reformasi; Heroes of the Reformation, an allusion to Indonesia's official pantheon of martyred independence and revolutionary fighters.

Later in the afternoon Monica left the rally to eat a snack at a noodle stall, then wandered around, weary of the speakers voicing noble, if identical, sentiments, but too upset to return to her studies. Near the campus perimeter, she noticed the street filling with scruffy-looking young men and other street people, the uneducated mob every middle-class Indonesian— Chinese or pribumi—alternately pities, despises, and fears. As the riot police watched, shields raised, several young men broke free from the front rank and hurled stones. When a driverless truck careened into the mob, scattering them in panic, Monica knew it was time to go home.

With no public transportation available, Monica walked home through the *kampung*, a warren of narrow streets, many mere pedestrian passageways, lying between the Trisakti campus and Monica's affluent neighborhood. The word *kampung* means village; its common usage to describe low-income neighborhoods in metropolitan Jakarta illustrates the tendency of lower-income pribumi Indonesians to cling to rural customs and manners in the city. The houses, though small and cramped, are well maintained within the limits of available resources and always tidy, reflecting their occupant's dignity and pride at being able to carve out a comfortable niche in the teeming capital. With little interior space to spare, life spills into the alleyways. Doors and windows remain open from dawn until late evening, offering passers-by intimate glimpses of family life. As in a village, the well-mannered simply avert their eyes, as they would passing a group of sarong-clad women bathing on a riverbank.

Monica rarely entered these narrow streets. Like most affluent Jakarta residents, she seldom walked anywhere in a city where a few steps in the afternoon heat leaves one drenched with perspiration, and sidewalks are an obstacle course of potholes and sizzling grease from roadside food stalls. She felt a faint sense of unease as the traffic sounds fell away and she entered the world of the pribumi. Although on a public footpath, she was careful to murmur apologies as she passed kampung residents sitting in the cool outside their homes or sipping coffee at a hole-in-the-wall café, and to preface requests for directions through the labyrinthine passageways with a respectful greeting. On the other hand, Monica avoided making eye contact with a half-dozen teenage boys lounging at the intersection of two pathways, ignoring the casual derisory comments and sneering laughter as she walked deeper into the kampung.

While Monica was navigating the unfamiliar route through the kampung, I was attempting to approach the heart of the unrest, spending a second frustrating afternoon trying to reach the Trisakti campus. I cooperated with the well-equipped graphic arts faculty to bring in and supervise graphic design projects to provide practical experience to senior students. These projects included several annual shareholder's reports for public-listed local companies, which had to be submitted to the local stock exchange in a few weeks time. While preparing these annual reports is a confusing, disorganized process at the best of times, the volatility of the rupiah had thrown many companies into total disarray. Because of an accounting system unequal to the task of monitoring multi-currency transactions, one client had only now discovered the company had lost money instead of raking in a windfall profit. I was compelled to rewrite large parts of the text to reflect the new situation. Though these projects were intended as an introduction to the high-pressure working environment of a commercial graphic design production house, I did not wish to ask students to re-do work when they were already burdened by upcoming examinations as well as by class disruptions caused by the demonstrations. I elected to make the changes myself.

The previous day, expecting a peaceful, controlled demonstration carried out according to the rules, I had asked my taxi driver to take the multi-lane expressway running past the campus. Even if access roads were blocked, I reasoned, the driver could drop me off at the toll gate a hundred meters south of my destination. When the shots rang out at Trisakti, I was sitting a traffic gridlock near that toll gate. Helpless, the driver and I listened to a radio station broadcasting continuous live reports from students and other bystanders using their cell phones to call the station from the scene. With disbelief turning to horror, we heard hysterical reports, later disproved, of police driving into the crowd on trail bikes, shooting indiscriminately. The driver turned off his meter and forbade me to leave the cab, insisting he was responsible for my safety until I reached my destination. By the time the gridlock had dissolved I had abandoned any intention of working that afternoon. Instead, I asked the driver to drop me off at my favorite pub.

My attempt to reach Trisakti the following day was no more successful. Besides completing my project, I was anxious to hear the accounts of my friends on campus and to attend the rally. But the taxi driver refused to consider approaching the general area, as his fellow drivers reported that large, unruly crowds were gathering in front of the campus. I gave up and returned to my rented room.

While watching the day's events on television I saw a presenter break into tears as she answered telephone calls and read faxes from appalled viewers. I realized then the Trisakti students I often dismiss as shallow, materialistic proto-Indoyups had touched the heart of a nation.

The following day, Jakarta leapt into global attention, competing only with an Indian nuclear test and the death of Frank Sinatra for headline space and leads on the television news. The mob of unemployed youths on the streets around Trisakti had initiated an escalating wave of vandalism. Although Monica was in the geographic heart of the unrest, her neighborhood was deceptively quiet, as though it were a public holiday. Looking over the rooftops, however, Monica could see several pillars of smoke as whole blocks in widely scattered parts of the city simultaneously went up in flames, giving the erroneous but horrifying impression that the entire capital was a raging inferno.

While Monica showed excellent sense by remaining at home with her family, I dove into the midst of the action. A testy phone call from my client left no doubt that in his view incipient revolution was no excuse for missing a deadline. I had heard the first reports of disturbances when I dropped by a friend's office in downtown Jakarta, whose computer I often use to check my e-mail. The Indonesian staff clustered around a radio broadcasting on-the-spot reports while the receptionist cut black cloth into armbands signifying condolence for the Trisakti Pahlawan Reformasi and solidarity with the reformist movement. Though reports were not clear about exactly where the disturbances were taking place, everyone insisted I accompany their boss to presumed safety at his house in the expatriate enclave of Kemang, where high concrete walls and armed guards would offer protection against a rampaging populace.

Wearing our black armbands, we left the office, debating which route to take, as both alternatives involved major roads that might be blocked off. We chose Jalan Rasuna Said, the most direct route.

Emerging from the side road, we expected panicked crowds and riot police. To our considerable surprise, nothing seemed to be amiss. A newspaper vendor tried to sell me an overpriced copy of *The Jakarta Post* as we edged into the traffic. I looked around and saw no indication that this was anything but a normal business day.

I weighed my options. Spending a presumably safe and pleasant afternoon lounging at my friend's backyard pool would probably cost me the contract. As a foreigner engaged in a slightly dubious deal for cut-rate commercial design, I had little control over my work and no legal recourse for broken agreements. With production houses begging for work in the devastated economy, my client could easily find another outfit to finish the job, thereby avoiding paying the remainder of my fee.

Apologizing to my friend, I stepped out of the slow-moving car and looked for a taxi. None were in sight, so I hailed a passing *ojek*, an insanely dangerous form of transport which involves clinging to the pillion seat of a motorcycle as a young man with minimal driving skills weaves through Jakarta's chaotic traffic with blithe disregard for the most elementary safety precautions. I was concerned the driver would refuse my request, but he enthusiastically agreed, claiming to be a demonstration veteran. Since the start of the student protests he assured me he had gained expertise carrying passengers to and from demonstrations, avoiding roadblocks and traffic with an impressive familiarity with Jakarta's tortuous network of alleys and footpaths.

There was little traffic to avoid as we headed north, then west. Along the way, I saw signs like protective talismans being posted on shuttered shops and buildings which stated that the establishment was pribumi-owned and supported the reform movement. The windows of the McDonald's on Jalan Thamrin were draped with banners proclaiming Islamic prayers. The Ramadan curtains, which shield good Muslims from the sight of infidels and apostates wolfing down cheeseburgers during the fasting month, were closed for good measure.

The direct-line route from the Jalan Thamrin McDonald's to Trisakti would take us through Tanah Abang, a bustling commercial and residential area. As we threaded our way through the back streets, I noticed few doorways that were open, which was highly unusual. All was quiet, save the clamor of our motorcycle echoing off the concrete walls of the tightly-packed kampung dwellings. Evidently, my driver's intimate knowledge of Jakarta streets did not include Tanah Abang. We suddenly emerged from the alleys onto the main commercial thoroughfare far from Trisakti—and stopped in our tracks. The street was empty of vehicles, save a few smoldering hulks. Hundreds of mostly young, shabbily dressed men milled in the street or rummaged through open shops. All the two- to four-story shop houses fronting the street were aflame or heavily damaged. It seemed every window on the lower floors was broken. The plate-glass façades of the banks were shattered, revealing the stained, chipped concrete underneath.

My first thought was, "Where did they get enough rocks to do that much damage?". I stepped off the machine and walked a few meters into the street for a better view. My driver called for me to return. When I did not reply, he turned around and roared back into

the alley, not waiting to be paid. I looked around but
saw no signs of riot police or any other authority. The
sensible course of action would have been to follow
my driver back into the alleys, perhaps to seek refuge
behind some closed door. But unlike my vanished
driver, I did not believe I was in any danger. The
rioters, mostly teenagers and young adults, either
ignored me or shouted an enthusiastic and friendly
"Hello, Mister!"—the common greeting for a foreigner.
Several gave me the thumbs-up signal on seeing my
black armband.

I banished all thoughts of my original destination
and began to walk north toward Glodok, Jakarta's
Chinatown, which seemed to be the heart of the
disturbance as most of the rioters were streaming from
that direction. I came upon a group of looters gleefully
distributing baked goods from the Dunkin' Donuts
shop. I had skipped breakfast that morning and was
in dire need of a caffeine and sugar hit myself, but I
could imagine security forces choosing just that
moment to appear and shoot me for possession of a
looted donut. As I continued northward I saw more
foreigners on the street. A couple of European
backpackers were taking participatory tourism to new
heights by joining looters cleaning out a compact disc
shop. One photojournalist, sensibly festooned with
press passes and cameras to announce his profession
and thus the legitimacy of his presence in a riot zone,
was engulfed by looters grinning for his camera.

I had almost reached Glodok when the military
finally rolled in. As the soldiers and police rounded
up straggling looters—and a number of innocent
bystanders—I continued northward to Kota, where I
witnessed the surreal spectacle at the Chicken Market

Bridge. Toward sunset I began the long walk home. With the city presumably under control, office workers joined me in my southward trek, many women forced to trudge several kilometers wearing spike-heeled office footwear. Some rioters did a quick turnover on their loot, selling toiletries and clothing to people who elected to stay the night camping out in their downtown office buildings.

Though I had felt perfectly safe in the midst of boisterous looters, as evening fell, I began to worry that I was an easy mark for professional criminals taking advantage of the general lawlessness. I decided to stay clear of the main roads and make my way home through residential neighborhoods, now barricaded and guarded by volunteer residents. As I passed access-road checkpoints the sentries applauded me for demonstrating solidarity in wearing the black armband, or maybe for my craziness in wandering alone through a city that the world now regarded as a war zone.

War Zone

DRIVING AROUND THE CITY with my friend Farid Baskoro the next day was a disturbing journey into a bizarre world in which the commonplace lay cheek-by-jowl with the horrific. Most of the city was untouched, seemingly normal except for the eerie absence of traffic and street peddlers. Then, turning a corner would reveal a scene of wholesale destruction.

Troops were standing guard on major street corners and in front of damaged shopping centers. Bystanders waved and cheered at the crews of armored personnel carriers patrolling the streets, particularly the Marines in their distinctive maroon berets. The Marines, like the rest of the navy, were widely regarded to be innocent of the oppressive excesses of the army and police during the three decades of Soeharto's rule.

Two days of riots had turned downtown Jakarta into a city holding its breath. Farid and I took full advantage of the empty streets, covering large areas of the city still open for vehicular traffic. We started our tour on Jalan Sudirman, the main north-south artery. From the news reports, we had expected some damage along the street, but the glass-walled skyscrapers, the most visible sign of Indonesia's prosperity and economic dynamism, were untouched.

At the presidential palace, now cordoned off, we were directed away from Jalan Hayam Wuruk, still littered with glass and debris. We made our way northward through side streets, detouring several times around streets barricaded by grim-faced residents clenching long wooden batons, until we reached Kota, where I had witnessed the line of looters crossing the Chicken Market Bridge the previous day.

I wanted to show Farid the heavy damage in Glodok, but we were directed away from the debris-strewn streets and still-smoldering buildings. Instead, we drove past Sunda Kelapa harbor, where we saw sailing schooners and colonial-era warehouses, relics of the days when the Dutch shipped nutmeg and cloves from the Spice Islands to Europe, and loaded coffee and rubber from plantations in the highlands south of Batavia onto four-masted clippers bound for destinations around the globe.

From there we continued eastward along the harbor road to the entry ramp of the elevated harbor-side toll road. Passing the unmanned toll booth, we drove up the ramp and along the deserted expressway toward Tanjung Priok, where the harbor toll road joins a similar elevated expressway going north to south. From this vantage point, we saw columns of concrete or glass-walled office, apartment, and hotel towers snaking through the expanse of single-story, red-tile-roofed residences, like an army advancing through conquered territory.

Farid and I ironically expressed our gratitude to "Tutut" Soeharto, the president's eldest daughter, for pushing through construction of these elevated expressways, which saved us the bother of picking our way through the debris-laden streets below. Of course, if the old man had not given his children free rein to plunder the nation, Farid and I probably would have been hard at work at our jobs on that bright morning, not surveying the post-apocalyptic scene of Jakarta after the riots. We left the toll road and drove westward toward Pasar Senen, a market area where Chinese- and pribumi-owned shops stand shoulder-to-shoulder. Now it was a patchwork of untouched shops standing serenely among the gutted remains of their neighbors.

We continued south, toward Kemang, my abortive destination of the previous day. In contrast to the districts we had previously toured, which had a large percentage of Chinese residents—severely damaged Glodok was almost entirely Chinese—the southern districts were pribumi country. Except for the most luxurious homes, owned mainly by Chinese, reflecting their predominance among the nation's economic elite, the southern districts were home mostly to Indonesians of ethnic Malay descent, who had inhabited the western islands of the Indonesian archipelago since ancient times.

Though Kemang and adjacent elite districts were untouched, looters had invaded the commercial blocks on the northern and eastern perimeters, many kilometers from the main centers of disturbance in the northern districts. Here, the damage was very selective, with banks and automobile showrooms taking the brunt of the destruction and looting.

After inspecting the surgical damage in the south we returned to the city center, our destination the Hotel Cemara, where Farid wanted to meet a journalist acquaintance who had arrived from Hong Kong to cover the riots. The Cemara, a budget-class business hotel close to the financial district and major government offices, was calling itself the "journalists' hotel," in imitation of wartime Saigon's Hotel

Continental. Today, the place was living up to its billing. Several times that afternoon a harried-looking photo-journalist or reporter would burst through the door and ask if Chinatown was still burning.

As we sipped our coffee, Farid, an avid and critical reader of international newsmagazines, voiced concerns about the slant and even the accuracy of the reports being filed by the international press corps members trading war stories at the other tables. Farid told me of listening to a breathless radio correspondent the previous evening proclaiming "fire is all around" in a vain attempt to sound like Walter Cronkite on the roof of the Continental or Peter Arnett leaning out the window of the Baghdad Hilton. News reports gave the impression that the entire city was in ruins, which was plainly not the case, as we had seen.

At the time, I thought Farid was overstating the case. The foreign journalists were not entirely to blame for presenting a sensationalistic view of Indonesian social unrest. One of the stories we heard in the Cemara coffee shop that afternoon was of an international news crew being stopped and threatened by an armed gang as they drove along the deserted toll road from the airport the previous night. The crew debated whether to open the trunk where they had stowed their camera equipment, as experience in these situations taught them that dissidents fighting an oppressive regime welcome global news coverage. If these rough-looking men wielding vicious *parang*—a type of machete—were grass-roots reformists, they would smile and wave the crew on with pleas to "tell the world our story." On the other hand, if they were bandits they would just run off with two hundred thousand dollars worth of television gear. The

Indonesian assistant who had met the crew at the airport talked with the marauders for a moment, then advised the producer to give their leader a hundred-dollar bill.

Sensationalistic or not, the journalists were covering a career-making story. According to official statistics published some months afterward, twenty-five hundred shop houses, forty shopping malls, a thousand residences, and over five hundred banks were damaged or burned during the riots. It was the worst instance of civil unrest in Jakarta's history.

Local television stations and newspapers carried graphic images of hundreds of charred corpses in burned-out shopping malls. Eyewitnesses told of looters rushing into burning buildings to grab as much as they could, regardless of personal safety. Stories emerged of Chinese Indonesians and people who simply looked Chinese assaulted in the streets.

Two days later, as I savored my first capuccino since the riot, the American newsreader on the television set suspended from the ceiling of the café announced "Jakarta Shops Closed for the Fourth Day." This was definitely news to me. Blok M shopping mall in South Jakarta, where the café was located, was teeming, with shoppers waiting ninety minutes in supermarket check-out lines. On this Sunday afternoon, three days after the riots, Jakartans had begun to venture out. While many of the sizable Christian population went to church for spiritual relief, others sought more material solace in the shops and supermarkets not destroyed in the riots.

I shrugged and returned to the futile task of making sense of my shopping receipts. Even before the riots, keeping track of expenses had become a futile endeavor as the crisis-fed inflation picked up steam. But as I was sipping coffee on that pleasant Sunday afternoon, the crisis and the events of the previous cataclysmic week seemed as distant as the foreign conflicts flitting across the television news. True, an armored personnel carrier guarded the main gate of the shopping mall, but when I passed the vehicle and poked my head inside, I saw the crew dozing peacefully. In the café, every table was full of laughing, relaxed families. This was Soeharto's Jakarta, as it had been for decades.

For Monica and many of Jakarta's ethnic Chinese community, however, the news reports were brutal reality. The day after the riots, friends and family phoned Monica's home to tell stories of shops looted and burned. These were small businesses, owned by people much like Monica's family. Though not poor, many had their entire life savings invested in the business, where they worked long and hard. For them, it was a devastating blow.

Most disturbing for Monica were widespread rumors of mass rape of ethnic Chinese women.

"None of my friends actually knew anyone who had been assaulted, but we didn't doubt the stories for a minute," Monica told me later. "No Chinese woman would admit to being raped. And besides, everyone was told that the rapists would go after anyone who talked."

Monica remained at home until Sunday, when she accompanied her family to church and then went grocery shopping and lingered over a long lunch. Many other Chinese Indonesians also ventured out that day.

Unlike Monica and her family, they had only one destination in mind: Soekarno-Hatta International Airport. Some tried to procure seats commercial carriers or chartered evacuation flights, others only sought refuge in the well-guarded facility.

The ethnic Chinese exodus was to last for weeks. Some, like the resident expatriates evacuated by their employers, treated the occasion as a holiday in Singapore, Australia, or Hong Kong. Others leaving behind razed homes or shattered businesses were unsure whether they would see the archipelago again.

Though many of her friends and neighbors were flying out, Monica had not considered leaving until Sunday evening, when a relative, "Uncle" Liem, phoned to offer her a ticket to Australia. Some distant relations in Sydney were eager, almost insistent, on giving Monica a safe home for an indefinite period.

"Uncle" Liem was actually a distant cousin of her mother who had frequent contact with the family through business ventures with her father. Unlike Monica's family, who were Christian and spoke only Indonesian, Liem's family were *totok* Chinese, a group who spoke Chinese and kept close ties with traditional Chinese culture. Although both families had lived in Indonesia for generations, their lifestyles were distinct. Monica's family lived in an ethnically mixed middle-class neighborhood, their home—save a few cans of pork in the kitchen cabinet—indistinguishable from those of their pribumi neighbors.

In contrast, Liem, an affluent bachelor, lived with his parents in Glodok, a wholly Chinese neighborhood seemingly transported intact from Hong Kong or Beijing. Monica's parents urged her to accept the offer.

She could already speak passable English, and most Australian universities had well-established procedures for accepting Asian students. If she wanted, Monica could slip into Australian life without undue difficulty.

Monica was hesitant. Though Liem took great pleasure in lavishing gifts on his many putative nieces and nephews, Monica often felt uncomfortable accepting his largesse. Monica disliked many aspects of totok life and customs, particularly the manner totok Chinese like Liem treated their pribumi employees.

"I remember one time he was taking my Mom and me to a wedding," Monica told me. "I was so embarrassed when he yelled at his driver for taking a wrong turn. The poor man, it was not his fault. It was raining hard and the street wasn't marked properly. It was even worse at his factory. When he didn't yell at his employees he treated them like children."

Nevertheless, Monica's parents and brother insisted she accept Liem's assistance. Monica was too well-mannered to refuse.

However, getting her on a flight the next day posed several difficulties. Unlike many Chinese Indonesians, who keep valid travel documents ready in anticipation of events like the recent riots, Monica, who had not yet traveled outside of Indonesia, had never considered applying for a passport. Early Monday morning Liem accompanied her to the local immigration office, where they encountered frenzy, chaos, and despair as hundreds of ethnic Chinese people clamored for service. Avoiding the motionless queues, Liem approached a clerk and spoke to him briefly, in a low voice. The clerk nodded, and told Liem and Monica to proceed behind the counter to a back office.

The senior immigration officer they met was friendly and polite. After asking a few perfunctory questions and inspecting Monica's identity documents and photographs, all the while nodding in official approval, he asked Monica to wait outside, so he and Liem could chat. A few minutes later, Liem emerged, looking satisfied. He suggested that they have lunch at a nearby hotel, as Monica's passport would not be ready for two hours.

The menu in the hotel coffee shop was festooned in hand-written strips of tape, as prices were altered almost daily to reflect the plummeting value of the rupiah. Monica, shocked at the cost of imported food, requested fried rice. Liem admonished her to accustom herself to Western cuisine. She acquiesced, and let Liem order her a club sandwich.

Over lunch, Monica told Liem he should not have spent so much money. She had heard that a new passport cost more than a thousand dollars. Liem told her not to worry. "These pribumi only understand money," he explained, patiently, as to a child. "We make it, we give some to them, they leave us alone. It is the way of things here."

Monica received her passport, packed, took a tearful leave of her parents, and went with Liem to the airport. They walked into scenes of bedlam as whole families besieged harried counter personnel or camped out on the terminal floor, waiting for nonexistent empty seats on the few flights not canceled because of the disturbances. Again, Liem ignored the queues and approached an airline official. After a brief conversation, he was ushered into a back office.

Monica did not consider herself an especially brave person, and certainly not a forceful or rebellious one.

Her parents were not overly strict; she could go wherever and with whomever she pleased. Now they were asking her to do something for her own good. But she did not feel comfortable taking Liem's money and enriching petty officials.

She looked around at the other would-be evacuees, who yelled imprecations or whispered to airline employees, hunching over with the conspiratorial look that indicated money was about to change hands. At one end of the terminal, she saw other families, some squabbling with their children, others gazing into space with fearful eyes. These, a woman told her, were Chinese people living nearby who sought refuge in the airport. For them, evacuation was a dream. They could only wait for a chance to return home, if their homes still existed.

"I felt if I left, I would never come back," Monica told me several weeks later. "I am proud of being Chinese, of my fair skin and my family's ability to work hard and save money. But I am also Indonesian. I don't speak Chinese and know nothing of Chinese history or culture. I was afraid that if I moved to Australia, my Indonesian-ness might just fade away, and I would be left with nothing I could call my own."

Liem reappeared, beaming and waving a ticket. As he picked up her bag and motioned for Monica to follow, she reached out and took Liem's arm. Eyes downcast, in a low voice, she told him she would prefer to return home.

Lengser Keprabon

WHILE MONICA NIBBLED on her overpriced sandwich and waiting for her passport, her fellow students returned to action. Like most Jakartans, student activists had laid low during the riots, many shocked by the forces they had apparently unleashed. With the situation seeming to stabilize on Monday, students from almost every university in the capital assembled at the campus of the University of Indonesia, the nation's most prestigious academic institution. Just before noon the students were bused, under military escort, to the MPR, the destination of the Trisakti demonstrators seven days before.

The MPR, the abbreviation for *Majelis Permusyawaratan Rakyat,* the People's Consultative Assembly, is the ostensible heart of Indonesia's democratic government, the venue for meetings of public representatives under Indonesia's quasi-parliamentary system. At the time I was living in a boarding house located a short distance from the MPR complex. When a friend working with a foreign news crew called me to say the buses were en route, I rushed outside and flagged an ojek. Unlike the over-confident driver of the previous Thursday, this driver was fully familiar with the route, delivering me to the MPR just as the students were disembarking from the buses and gathering in front of a phalanx of military riot troops.

I hung back, literally gun-shy, half-expecting a replay of the previous week's tragedy at Trisakti, as the students pushed against the massed riot shields. On this occasion, however, after offering token resistance, several soldiers stepped aside, letting a handful, then a steady stream, of students pass the barricades and enter the MPR grounds.

I felt this occasion was more theatre than serious confrontation. The soldiers' initial resistance and subsequent retreat struck me as similar to ritual performances common in most Indonesian cultures, where personal or community events are announced through clearly defined, stylized action. In this case, perhaps, the soldiers acknowledged their duty by initially resisting the students, then displayed their sympathy for the student's cause by stepping aside.

I left the scene shortly afterward, worried that the actions of a few front-line soldiers might not be official policy. I did not relish being trapped inside the MPR grounds if the military had a sudden change of heart.

At the de facto heart of Indonesian sovereignty, soon-to-be-former President Soeharto struggled to maintain his position as the vultures gathered around the stately neo-classical presidential palace on the north side of Merdeka Square. Soeharto had cut short his attendance at an international summit in Egypt following the riots, arriving home to a subdued reception on Saturday. While in Egypt, Soeharto had indicated that he would resign if the Indonesian people so desired. Soeharto used the phrase *lengser keprabon*, the Javanese term for the abdication of a king, as if finally confirming the widely held perception he was less a modern president than a feudal monarch.

After issuing pro-forma threats to crack down on students, rioters, communists, and other perennial threats to the social order, Soeharto tried to make sense of this appalling turn of events. Exactly what happened behind the scenes prior to his resignation will probably never be known. Soeharto gave few interviews in his life, and none after his fall from power. All descriptions of his words and actions during his final days, except for brief appearances on television, are second- or third-hand. Many of these reports from various sources portray a tired, elderly man who sincerely wanted to step aside but was misled by underlings and pressured by family and friends to continue protecting their business interests.

According to some reports, Soeharto reserved special opprobrium for Harmoko, his former Minister of Information and among his most loyal supporters for over two decades. Soeharto complained the information he had received from Harmoko was about as accurate as the blatant lies perpetrated by the Department of Information. Earlier in the year, Harmoko had assured Soeharto that Indonesians, from the Jakarta suburbs to remote villages, wanted their seventy-seven-year-old president to accept a seventh five-year term.

Now parliamentary speaker, Harmoko jolted the nation on Monday afternoon by announcing the decision taken by the legislature to ask Soeharto to resign. Some observers speculated Harmoko had finally lost patience when passed over for the vice presidency two months before, others surmised he was annoyed at being the only minister to have his personal residence destroyed by fire during the riots.

On Tuesday morning Farid and I were having coffee and reading the morning papers in his "command post," a room in his house he had converted into an office, where news blared from both the radio and television while a computer connected to the Internet displayed real-time situation updates. A report that President Soeharto had called a group of Muslim leaders to draft a program for governmental reform caused Farid to sputter out a mouthful of coffee.

Though Farid was Muslim he was appalled at the news, worried that Soeharto was scheming to stay in power by forming an alliance with fundamentalist Islamic leaders. We soon discovered, to our relief, that Soeharto had actually summoned moderate Muslim intellectuals—who all espoused the wisdom of separating mosque from state in a multi-ethnic society like Indonesia—to draft an outline for a reform committee.

The government-owned television network was broadcasting live from the State Palace. On the television screen, Soeharto was an aged, forlorn figure as he waited in an anteroom for reform committee members. When the participants finally arrived and the doors closed the government television network switched to pre-recorded performance of *keroncong*, a lilting, polyrhythmic music form popular with older Indonesians. Farid and I were annoyed, as though CNN had cut away from live broadcast of a breaking news event to cover a polka concert.

Though the meeting was scheduled for twenty minutes, viewers had to endure almost two-hours of keroncong before Soeharto and the others reappeared. As usual, he showed no emotion as he read the prepared text of the reform package to the nation. Most observers suspected the plan, which called for fresh elections in which Soeharto would not run, was nothing more than a ploy to buy time for the Soeharto family and friends to cash out and move their money to safe havens overseas.

Later reports indicated such a cynical view might have been unwarranted. Several participants of the reform committee meeting claimed that Soeharto frequently sighed "*Saya bosan jadi presiden,*" I'm tired of being president. Whether these were the sincere feelings of a man exhausted by three decades of presidential burden or yet another crafty ploy from an acknowledged master of dissimulation will never be known. Farid showed me a newspaper story reflecting his own opinion. The headline, which would have had the publication banned and the editors jailed six months before, proclaimed "The President Has Lost His Way."

From Farid's house I went to the MPR, where the students seemed to be in command. A carnival atmosphere reigned. Soldiers were chatting with protesters, children sat on armored personnel carriers, and food hawkers did a roaring trade. Beggars roamed the crowd gathered outside the gates, the more light-fingered found foreign journalists easy picking for cell phones and portable computers. Though the military controlled the area outside the MPR perimeter, the students determined who could enter the complex itself. Somewhat officiously, one of the gatekeepers demanded identification when I approached the gate. I had neglected to bring any ID, so I searched through my tote bag, finding a long-expired Canadian driver's license, which seemed to do the trick.

Inside the venue, firebrands from social-political faculties gave colorful denunciations of Soeharto and cronies to eager foreign reporters, their charming, idiosyncratic English masking a shaky grasp of history, economics, and politics. After talking for a few hours with the students I discovered that the scene, though euphoric, had little depth. Repeated questions about the student's program and agenda elicited no further response than a desire to see an end to Soeharto's rule with no clear concept of how to replace the existing authoritarian government with a more democratic political system.

Monica was also at the MPR. All day Monday Monica's phone had rung with further reports of rapes and murders of Chinese women. Monica's mother cried on several occasions, viewing Monica's decision not to evacuate with mixed emotions. Monica's efforts to console her only resulted in them weeping together.

A phone call on Tuesday morning from Nina, her pribumi friend, offered Monica an escape. As Nina's parents had forbid her to go to the MPR alone, she implored Monica to accompany her.

Monica was once again torn between her family duty and her own desires. Although she knew her parents were concerned, with much justification, for her safety, she was tiring of the fearful atmosphere at home. Eventually her parents gave grudging consent. On impulse she grabbed the Nikon camera "Uncle" Liem had given her the year before and walked out the door, where Nina waited with her father.

Nina's father drove the pair to within a few hundred meters of the MPR, where a police blockade was turning back most vehicular traffic. After a final assurance to Nina's father that they would not take chances and return home at a reasonable hour, Nina and Monica alighted from the vehicle and proceeded on foot through the milling crowd to the MPR gate.

Monica smiled as she passed a mineral water vendor explaining to an amused audience that Soeharto needed his product more than anyone, as the embattled leader was constantly wetting his trousers in terror of losing the presidency. In response to an invitation from a young woman near the end of a line of marching students, Monica and Nina joined the group, each grasping the thin nylon rope intended to keep the group members in loose formation. Safely amid their fellow students, the two friends passed through the gauntlet of troops to enter the impromptu carnival inside the complex.

After passing through the gauntlet of student security at the main gate, Monica and Nina proceeded to a makeshift stage near the administration building, where they listened to alternately humorous and haranguing speeches by reformist politicians and student activist leaders.

Monica felt out of place. She saw few other Chinese Indonesians, and again felt the usual unease of a Chinese person amid a large group of pribumi. Monica realized the futility of planning an escape route; the only exit was the blocked and guarded main gate. To calm her nerves, Monica began to photograph the colorful scene, paying close attention to the interaction between the students and troops as they chatted, swapped cigarettes, and shared fried snacks and sweet cakes.

Elsewhere, away from the presidential palace, which was now cordoned by armored troops, and the riot-torn blocks where cleanup crews were still finding burned bodies in the ruins, city life carried on as though it were a minor holiday. Bored with the monotonous MPR scene, I left the compound and wandered through the downtown alleyways, watching ordinary people filling the day with domestic chores or conversations at the neighborhood warung. Though one subject dominated most social gatherings, there was little passion or polemic. While the military and political elite frantically maneuvered for position, Jakartans sat back and enjoyed the show.

The troops guarding strategic intersections and public buildings were unfailingly polite, listening patiently to students and social activists—now coming out of the woodwork by the hundreds—who harangued them about their civic duty.

But fear and tension remained. At sunset, I dropped into one of the city's top hotels for the best "Happy Hour" deal in Jakarta: the expatriate manager was offering a free beer to all foreigners who could prove they had remained in Jakarta during the riots. Sitting with another long-time foreign resident, who had earned a second free beer for actually flying in on the night of the riots, we heard the manager relating how the hotel's owner had panicked at the sight of his lobby teeming with Chinese Indonesians who had sought refuge in his hotel.

The refugees, who had pushed the hotel's occupancy rate from ten percent to a hundred-and-ten percent overnight, were clearly visible from the street through the floor-to-ceiling plate-glass windows. He told the manager to restrict all Chinese-featured guests to internal areas of the hotel. Aware his boss intended to cancel his dollar-based contract in order to hire an Indonesian at a much-lower salary, the manager decided to go out in style. Knowing his boss liked to give his hotel colonial airs—believing a recreation of nineteenth-century Java to be the height of sophistication—the manager posted an authentic Dutch-era sign, which might have appeared in a stately colonial hotel a century ago: "No Chinese or Dogs Allowed in Lobby."

With most other entertainment venues being closed and unwilling to spend the evening in my dingy rented room, I stayed in the hotel for a few more beers and dinner, walking the short distance home shortly before midnight, along streets deserted except for military convoys. The next morning, the city finally began to resemble the lurid descriptions in the international reports. Merdeka Square, the kilometer-square public park flanked by the presidential palace and major government and military buildings, was sealed with barbed-wire barricades; tanks stood guard, their gun barrels aimed straight down deserted Jalan Thamrin.

After breakfast, I decided to walk to the MPR. I emerged from my neighborhood alleyway onto Jalan Sudirman, about two kilometers south of Merdeka Square. Here, as well, the main thoroughfare was devoid of any traffic, including pedestrians. I asked a soldier if I might be permitted to cross the street. The soldier broke into a grin, inviting me to walk down the middle of the road if I wished.

Despite the show of force, good manners and relaxed attitudes seemed to be the order of the day. At the MPR front gate, Permadi, an astrologer jailed by Soeharto some years before for predicting the President's downfall, sat on the roof of his car, using a megaphone with an Indonesian mystic's practiced showmanship to request passage from military guards.

I decided not to enter the noisy, boisterous MPR grounds again, preferring to wander the streets of the quiet capital under clear skies. Monica and Nina, however, returned to the MPR and spent the rest of the day watching and photographing the university groups, who marched around the complex grounds in colorful processions, staged street theater performances, and burned government figures in effigy. Class clowns vied for the honor of representing Soeharto as, tongues wagging and eyes bulging, they dangled on imaginary hangman's ropes.

Their caricatures of the only national leader they had ever known were not far off the mark. A frenzy of palace intrigues and political positioning had left the modern-day sultan twisting in the wind. Soeharto announced his resignation just after nine a.m. Thursday, coincidentally a national holiday commemorating the founding of one of the first organizations promoting Indonesian self-determination. Vice president B.J. Habibie was sworn in as president immediately afterward. After giving Habibie, his long-time protégé, an enigmatic half-smile, Soeharto turned and walked from the palace he had occupied for three decades.

President Habibie's inaugural speech that evening closed those terrible ten days on a note of farce. After years of Soeharto's reassuring, avuncular figure on our television screens, we were treated to the diminutive figure of the nation's third president almost lost behind a vast expanse of desktop. As I watched the new head of state stumble through his maiden speech to the nation he now led, I imagined a ten-year-old having his photo taken at his father's office. Memories of a personal meeting with Habibie several years before, when he had sat in a similar executive office chair, only reinforced this impression. Then, and most likely now, his feet did not reach the floor.

Café Society

"Be careful with what you wish for" was pertinent advice for Indonesians thrust into the reform era after Soeharto resignation. Having gained what they had fervently desired for years, and actively sought for months, they were left, stunned and blinking, in a new, uncharted world.

Many were traumatized by the loss of the reassuring father figure who had dominated their newspapers and television screens for three decades. A few political observers questioned the wisdom of summarily dismissing the old man only to replace him with Habibie, no one's idea of a national leader.

To be fair, the new president did get off to a good start. Although Habibie did not invite reformist figures to join his cabinet, the predominance of respected academics and technocrats over the sycophants and opportunists found in later cabinets helped to curtail initial criticism.

But the attempt to return to normal life only brought the realization that Krismon, as the Indonesians termed the economic crisis which had precipitated Soeharto's fall, showed no signs of abating. Attempts by the media and economic notables to foster a crisis mentality were met with vague responses from the government and total indifference from the public. As one observer noted in July: "Krismon will be over in six months, because by then it will be 'Krismas.'"

While most Indonesians descended into apathy and denial, I retreated into fantasy, specifically my college-days dream of living in Berlin during the years following the First World War. My fascination with Berlin during the Weimar Republic stemmed in part from the vibrant, pioneering art such as the socialist theater of Bertholt Brecht, expressionist films like *Nosferatu* and *Metropolis* as well as the legendary demi-monde memorably portrayed in *The Blue Angel*. But I was even more intrigued by economic conditions during the mid-twenties. Sharing a damp basement suite with three other students in Canada, I read of my counterparts a half century earlier buying luxury apartments and automobiles with their dollar-based allowances.

Punitive reparation payments to the victorious nations had, along with other factors, pole-axed the German economy in the years after the war. Feverish printing of money to meet payments and keep the economy running spawned one of history's more spectacular episodes of hyperinflation. Prices and wages rose daily. By 1924, the dollar was worth four quadrillion marks and suitcases had replaced wallets as repositories of cash. On payday, Germans dashed to stores to buy provisions for the week, as the quantity of money sufficient to purchase enough bread to feed a family on Friday could barely buy a cookie the following Tuesday.

German-style hyperinflation seemed a serious

possibility when Indonesia followed other East Asian skyrocketing economies as they aborted their trajectories and plummeted to earth. A decade-long frenzy of debt-fueled, unregulated industrial growth had built a glittering edifice of economic development largely unsupported by requisite financial or legal foundations.

In July 1997 the hoary old domino theory of serial toppling governments in East Asia became a reality. This time, it was not shadowy communist subversives but staunchly capitalist currency speculators who sparked social and political unrest throughout the region. That month, the free market sharks launched their strike at the soft underbelly of the "Asian Economic Miracle," the overvalued national currencies undermined by a lopsided balance of foreign payments and huge offshore debts. The Thai baht was the first to fall, Indonesia's fragile currency followed six weeks later as the rupiah began a precipitous slide from 2,500 to the five-digit range, briefly touching 17,000 to the American dollar in January 1998 before crawling back up to 12,000. As the price of imports soared out of reach, the Indonesian economy went into shock, all save the most essential transactions deferred until someone could figure out what the hell was going on.

Although the inflation in Indonesia was not as severe, I fancied I could detect numerous parallels between Jakarta in the nineties and Weimar Berlin. During both periods, those fortunate enough to possess dollars or other solid currencies found a sybarites' dream. Anything from a sinful night on the town to a fully appointed yacht was available for derisory sums. True aficionados of the period, like myself, could take a virtual visit to Weimar Berlin by taking a taxi north to the remnants of colonial Batavia near the Jakarta waterfront, where a Dutch-era warehouse had been rebuilt into an authentic Berlin café. Stepping onto Taman Fatahillah, the town square during the early colonial period, all signs of modern Jakarta vanished, replaced by a nineteenth-century European town. During the late evening I would walk across the square, flanked by brooding neo-classical buildings, avoiding the beggars, hustlers, and prostitutes who grew more numerous with each passing week, before stepping through the fine mahogany doors into a world of decadent, bohemian splendor. I would perch on a bar stool and observe the polyglot assembly of free-spending foreigners, eccentric artists, ravishing bar girls, and equally ravishing transvestites, with a dispassionate, analytical eye: "I am a Digital Camera." I could play my fantasy to the hilt until, in the early hours, I asked for the bill. Comparing the six-digit tab with the meager contents of my wallet confirmed I was indeed living in Weimar Berlin—as a German.

Earning only rupiah—and not many at that—I found that aspects of daily life I once took for granted had become unaffordable luxuries. Cheese, yogurt, and other European staple foods became as extravagant as a diet of champagne and caviar. Even the American fast food I usually disdain was far beyond my budget. Worst of all, after a long, hot day of futile efforts to drum up business or chase down payments, I could no longer retreat to the cool interior of my favorite Australian-style pub, where excellent draft beer awaited in a frosted glass. I could only squeeze onto the crowded wooden bench of a *warung*—a type of makeshift roadside food stall found throughout Indonesia—and sip an *es teler*, a shaved-ice concoction slathered with sweet condensed milk and brightened by syrup that comes in the color of neon signs.

Of course, all economic circumstances are relative. For me, a quadrupling in price of my favorite imported cheese was an inconvenience. For a middle-class mother, the four-fold increase in baby formula and other products needed by a growing family was a serious concern. Further down the economic scale, mothers fed their weaned infants rice water, which alleviated hunger pangs but provided minimal nutrition.

The most worrisome concern for Jakarta's newly-impoverished middle-class was not the soaring price of essential needs. The plunging rupiah had driven the cost of a night on the town beyond the budgets of most Indoyups. This was serious. Indonesians are a highly sociable people, and they love to display their wealth. The café scene had provided ample opportunity for Jakartans to express both characteristics during the boom years. When I first moved to Jakarta, the stock answer to the question "Where is the best place to go at night?" was "Singapore." By the mid-nineties, the explosive economic growth had fueled the emergence of a nightlife that, if not exactly on a par with London, Paris, or New York, was a long way from the kampung. Krismon almost killed Jakarta's café society, as once-affluent clientele were no longer able to pay outrageous prices for watery cappuccino or ersatz western food. As the crisis continued, the prices rose further as many cafés were located in downtown office buildings or elite-district houses, where rent payments are generally tied to the prevailing exchange rate of the American dollar.

The café scene deteriorated further as television

stars, pop singers, and other celebrities could no longer enliven a favorite nightspot with their glittering presence. The general decline in consumer purchasing power and the unstable rupiah had sent the advertising industry into a corporate coma. With almost all advertising campaigns halted, television stations could no longer afford to air local programs, which rely on sharing advertising revenue with the producers. Some of the most famous faces in the land joined the growing army of unemployed. Few could afford to remain idle for an indefinite period. Most minor and a few top celebrities saw their savings diminish with no new prospects in sight. Rather than wail and wring their hands in anguish—though most had had extensive practice at both in television melodramas—they followed the same course as any Indonesian in dire financial straits: they opened restaurants.

Every evening, millions of Indonesians wheel pushcarts to strategic locations in city centers and suburban crossroads and set up rudimentary restaurants. Some of the best food in Indonesia is found in these humble street-side stalls, as demonstrated by the luxury sedans often parked beside warung with established reputations. During Krismon, many of these flashy vehicles belonged to the owners themselves, as the newly unemployed celebrities opened up their own distinctive food stalls, dubbed *kafé tenda*.

Leafy suburban avenues became raucous carnivals as late-model sport utility vehicles arrived and disgorged the components of these instant cafés. The result resembled a cross between a wine bar and a hot dog stand. All tried, with varying success, to create a distinctive atmosphere. Some were romantic, or just very badly lit. Most offered nothing more than basic fried food, sweet fruit-juice concoctions and the chance to meet a favorite over-the-hill leading man or vacuous starlet. Celebrity drawing power had turned the kafé tenda into the new centers of Jakarta night life.

One evening, I journeyed to Jalan Tirtayasa in the elite suburb of Kebayoran to check out Kafé Tirtayasa, the center of the kafé tenda scene. I found myself in a traffic jam reminiscent of boom-time Jakarta. Parking attendants were shouting contradictory directions to the drivers of vehicles vainly trying to enter the street. I slipped between the fenders and strolled along a boulevard lined with pastel-colored canvas awnings stretched on shiny aluminum frames, like a garden party in a well-to-do neighborhood.

One establishment caught my eye through the correct spelling of "spaghetti" and "cappuccino;" no mean feat in a country where attempts at foreign-language orthography range from risible to incomprehensible. I recognized the café name as that of a former movie scream queen, a genuinely beautiful woman with considerable charm who appeared in most films as a *kuntilanak*, a seductive incubus whose waist-length hair hides a gaping hole in her back. I tried to banish this disturbing image from my thoughts as I selected a table with a checkered tablecloth and candle guttering in the evening breeze. A well-groomed man in his mid-thirties, possibly the star's son, approached and asked for my order in fluent English.

Long experience ordering western food in small establishments—and several top hotels—taught me to hope for the best and fear the worst. I did not expect much beyond pallid noodles in tomato ketchup and

instant coffee with a dollop of canned whip cream, so
I was surprised and delighted to hear the unmistakable
bubbling roar of milk being steamed emanating from
the other side of the rattan screen separating the
dining area from the rudimentary kitchen. The waiter
reappeared bearing a designer coffee cup overflowing
with cinnamon-sprinkled foam. One sip proved this
was a decent cappuccino, made from arabica coffee and
fresh milk. A few minutes later the waiter set down a
plate of whole-wheat pasta with tuna and shellfish in
marinara sauce, and, it seemed, fresh basil. I dug in,
marveling I was enjoying a delicious Mediterranean
meal on a suburban Jakarta roadside.

When I had finished, the waiter cleared my table,
then returned to sit with me, uninvited. This is a
common occurrence in warung and small restaurants
in areas with few foreign visitors, but rare in Jakarta.
As I groped for words to protest this intrusion without
seeming rude, he introduced himself. His name was
Heri, the husband of the café owner, who, as it turned
out, was not the movie star but her daughter, Yani. I
was the first foreigner to visit his wife's café, and he
wanted my opinion. I offered heartfelt praise for the
delicious food. Aware many Indonesians feel it is
impolite to offer any sort of criticism, even if
specifically requested, I also tactfully pointed out a
few trivial deficiencies to demonstrate my sincerity.

Heri, in his mid-thirties, had the soft, indulged
face common in Indonesians of his age and class. Even
with an order pad in his hand, I could easily imagine
Heri in a spotless white Arrow shirt and Hugo Boss
tie, sitting behind the wheel of his BMW, one hand
carelessly on the steering wheel, the other holding the
latest-model cell phone to his ear.

I only missed that image by a few months. Until late 1998, Heri was a loan officer at a major private bank. His father was a chicken farmer, an astute businessman who had entered the poultry business just as the emerging middle class sent the demand for eggs and chicken soaring. Success allowed Heri's father to enroll his son in Trisakti University and subsequently send him to graduate school in the United States. Returning to Indonesia in 1990 with his freshly minted MBA, Heri began his career during the halcyon years of private banking, when deregulation opened the door to any wealthy Indonesian who wanted to park his Mercedes in front of his own bank. Heri's Trisakti connections soon landed him a junior management position in a private bank owned by a First Family associate. Within a year he was shoveling out money to borrowers whose chief qualification was a close relationship to a Soeharto family member or crony rather than proven business ability.

This was not the case, however, with one of his favored clients. In exchange for a full partnership, he secured a big loan to expand his father's chicken business. When I questioned the ethics, or even the legality of this arrangement, Heri only shrugged. I suppose he believes there is nothing wrong with nepotism as long as you keep it in the family.

Unlike most of his bank's clients, Heri and his father put the borrowed capital to good use, expanding equipment and facilities in step with market demand. Heri's numerous contacts from the banking industry led to new customers among the growing supermarket chains and fast-food outlets. Heri also introduced enlightened management techniques and practices into this traditional business, with varying results.

Concerned his employees were eating their company-supplied lunch from discarded newspapers and sharing a few battered tin cups, Heri sought to improve hygiene—and, of course, to lower losses from sick days—by purchasing rugged, cafeteria-style plates and drinking cups for each worker. The gifts were accepted graciously. A few days later Heri noticed the employees were again eating from newspapers. His foreman explained the workers had carefully stored the brand-new lunch sets at home, so they could bring out the good plastic for guests.

"We felt like we were on top of the world," Heri told me. "I knew full well we were operating with no regulation or infrastructure. But we were making so much money. We thought the party would never end."

When the party did end Heri concentrated on maintaining the chicken farm. But the near-collapse of the rupiah in January 1998 almost destroyed the chicken business. With most broiler feed imported, the cost of raising the chickens soared out of reach. After two months of enormous losses, feeding the animals grass and scraps, his father ordered the remaining chickens slaughtered and sold, then closed the farm, as did many of his competitors. While newspapers sounded dire warnings of a land without chickens, Heri returned to the bank, which was now in total disarray. With no new lending and few debtors willing or even able to make loan payments, Heri had no reason to come to the office, especially after his paychecks stopped. He struggled to stay afloat, making regular trips to the pawnshop with jewelry and other accouterments of past affluence. All, of course, except his cell phone. He would rather lose a body part than give up his cell phone, though he could only afford to use it for incoming calls.

Living close to Kebayoran, Heri and Yani witnessed the start of the kafé tenda phenomenon. They immediately saw the potential. Though long retired, Yani's mother had a wide following of loyal fans. She was also becoming known to the young as television stations, unable to afford imported programs, were filling up air time by plundering Indonesia's extensive stock of horror movies. Yani's mother agreed to finance the venture on one condition, that the enterprise would be Yani's alone. She did not trust her formerly high-flying son-in-law to handle the business.

The kafé tenda was an immediate success, although Yani's mother, a Garboesque recluse in recent years, never once made an appearance. Heri helped out on busy nights, or when Yani attended to other business. He occasionally brooded as he counted the meager revenue, remembering the days when he would spend in one night what was now the take for an entire week. At least the café was paying the bills, a feat few of Heri's former colleagues could manage.

I became a Kafé Tirtayasa regular. A few days later, Heri introduced me to Yani. In designer T-shirt and jeans, charming and lively, speaking fluent, idiomatic American-accented English, Yani brought the grace and poise of an accomplished society hostess to this roadside warung. Heri's most notable contribution to the café was his beloved one-shot espresso maker, which, like his cell phone, did not follow the other Indoyup appliances to the pawnshop. Yani had charmed the owner of the house behind the café location to let them plug into his power outlet for a token payment. Heri, like me, believed that on the island that gave the world the word "java", to be unable to enjoy a decent cup of coffee was inconceivable.

Jaman Edan

I SPENT MY FIRST YEARS IN INDONESIA on the fringes of the journalist's trade, writing feature articles for regional magazines and reporting on the developing travel industry for business publications. Though several friends urged me to devote myself seriously to a journalism career—for the sake of a regular salary if nothing else—I routinely turned down offers to work as a stringer for newspapers and news magazines not operating a full bureau in Indonesia. I finally decided to drop any further journalistic endeavors soon after the publication of my second book, a lavishly illustrated travel guide with literary pretensions. One of Jakarta's then-small contingent of resident foreign correspondents congratulated me and sardonically suggested that my next effort should be a real book instead of glorified captions for glossy travel photos. He confided he would also like to write books, but his wire service had forced him to undergo a lobotomy before they promoted him to bureau chief.

He was selling himself short. Serious attempts at journalism during the New Order required a prodigious degree of subtlety, tact, and skill. A foreign correspondent transgressing the government's strict and ever-changing guidelines risked deportation.

Unlike local journalists, who faced loss of livelihood or worse when they tweaked the government's nose, some foreign journalists regarded deportation from Indonesia as a good career move. But editors knew anyone could get themselves summarily kicked out, if only for repeating in print the daily talk of the town.

The foreign correspondents whom editors respected and government officials tolerated were consummate professionals, dedicated to performing a difficult job under treacherous conditions. This bunch was a far cry from the bloated has-beens and swashbuckling hot shots portrayed in *The Year of Living Dangerously*, an imaginative novel about an Australian journalist set during the weeks before the attempted coup in September 1965. As the film adaptation was reasonably successful, I had often entertained the idea of writing a screenplay about Jakarta-based journalists in the 1990s. An acquaintance with film production experience dissuaded me: he could not see a property entitled *The Year of Playing It Safe* attracting much attention in Hollywood.

The downfall of Soeharto and subsequent relaxation of press controls brought journalists flocking to Jakarta. Farid often complained about what he regarded as the misrepresentation—bordering on sensationalism—of Indonesia in the foreign press. According to Farid, decades of willful obstruction and misinformation by the New Order government and current superficial reporting by the media stars and hordes of enthusiastic freelancers had created a misleading and damaging view of Indonesia in eyes of the world. Even long-time resident correspondents, who were generally familiar with Indonesia's complex society, history, and politics, did little to foster a fair and accurate representation. When all eyes were on Indonesia, such as during the May Riots, international celebrity correspondents shoved aside local reporters, a process known as "bigfooting." Farid feared Indonesia had become the most misunderstood nation on earth.

Farid convinced me that I could make a small but valuable contribution to repairing this damage and presenting a more accurate image of his nation to the world. Besides, he pointed out, I would realize a tidy sum when even minimal dollar-based fee payments were converted to devalued rupiah.

For me, struggling to maintain a decent standard of living, Farid's second point was more compelling. While I was willing to give reporting another go, I was unsure what sort of journalism I should pursue. My cavalier attitude to fact verification disqualified me from hard news, while Indonesia's pariah status in the travel industry had closed any market for travel writing, my erstwhile stock-in-trade.

I tried e-mailing some opinion pieces and personal observations to newspapers and magazines in my native Canada and elsewhere. Wanting to emphasize the positive, I concentrated on "good news:" the rapid return of normal life, the absence of a sense of crisis, and the fundamental tolerance and hospitality of Indonesians.

None were published, or even acknowledged, except for one scathing rejection from an editor who obviously had some time on his hands. In a message dripping with arch condescension, he forgave me for trying the old freelancer's trick of flogging feature articles for easy money though I had little familiarity with the subject. This only works, he said, if the writer does at least minimal research to add plausibility to descriptions of situations and events. My submission showed I was almost totally ignorant of the current situation in Jakarta, as my observations were so contradictory to reports published every day in the world media.

I read the message with mounting confusion until I realized I had submitted the piece using an e-mail account whose return address did not indicate I was physically in Indonesia. I suppose this is why he closed the message by admitting that the article, though fanciful, was quite readable. He invited me to try again with a more factual piece if I were ever to visit Indonesia.

My remaining opportunity to make some money through journalism was writing for trade publications, which are magazines and newspapers focusing on events, issues, and personalities in a specific industry. The work is, to be blunt, excruciatingly boring, as the writer is required to muster high enthusiasm for fascinating subjects like petrochemical refining and automotive spare parts.

Even in this field I had limited options. Besides resource extraction, fisheries, and agro-industry, all requiring costly travel, furniture exporting was the only business thriving during Krismon. After I received an expression of interest from the editor of an American home furnishings magazine, Farid suggested I visit an acquaintance who owned a small furniture shop in South Jakarta.

Pak Trisno's shop was located on a street lined with similar establishments. This is a common occurrence in Indonesia, as in many other countries. Foreigners are often amused seeing long ranks of market stalls or small shops selling exactly the same goods. They seldom realize that most small-scale commerce is based on personal contact. With credit, consumer rights, and other legal safeguards still undeveloped, buyers prefer to deal with specific merchants with whom they have an established relationship.

I had not visited Jalan Ciputat, the "antique furniture street," for several years. I remembered a long line of ramshackle shops filled to the rafters with moldy fake antiques, owners staring into the street with bored, sometimes almost forlorn, expressions in what seemed a futile wait for customers. I was surprised to see the street was now a bustle of activity, with trucks loading or unloading in front of almost every shop.

Pak Trisno's shop was large, well-lit and tidy, filled with teak and rattan furniture of fine material and craftsmanship. I saw a teenage boy dusting the merchandise with considerable industry. When he confirmed I was in Pak Trisno's establishment I asked him to fetch the proprietor.

Pak Trisno appeared through a doorway at the back of the shop. He appeared to be about seventy years old, and in good health. He was tall, even by Western standards, and lean, with a care-worn face set with lively, observant eyes. Evidently at ease around foreigners, he greeted me in English, with a warm smile.

I expected he would be disappointed to learn I had no intention of buying so much as an ashtray, but Pak Trisno's eyes lit up when I explained the purpose of my visit. He invited me to walk through the rear doorway, which led to a terrace at the edge of a lush, walled-in garden. As I took a seat on a comfortable

rattan chair trimmed with fine leather, I began to
suspect Pak Trisno kept the best pieces for himself.
He walked over to a large, brand-new refrigerator
humming in the corner. Opening the door, he asked
if I would prefer mineral water, a soft drink, or a bottle
of the imported beer he kept in stock for meetings with
his European buyers.

I spent the remainder of a very pleasant afternoon
in that garden. Only on two occasions did Pak Trisno
excuse himself briefly to deal with walk-in customers.
Most of his business was directly with foreign buyers;
much of the furniture on display was already sold. That
stock, and more scattered in warehouses around
Jakarta, was waiting for shipment, delayed for some
weeks now because of a shipping container shortage.
The collapse of the economy had reduced inbound
shipping to insignificant levels, and as a consequence
there were few empty containers on Indonesia's docks.

Remembering I was supposed to be interviewing
him for a business magazine piece, I asked Pak Trisno
what action he would take to deal with the high
inventory level and stalled business.

"I will sit back and relax," he told me. "Sooner or
later someone will realize they can make a huge profit
shipping empty containers to Indonesia, thereby
solving the problem."

His relaxed attitude seemed to confirm my
suspicion that Pak Trisno, for all his apparent
prosperity, was not primarily a businessman, or at least
not concerned with wringing the last drop of profit
from his business activities. As our conversation
drifted to other matters, I discovered Pak Trisno had
been a journalist. For the rest of the afternoon I
listened to the astounding and disturbing story of Pak

Trisno's journey from newspaper desk to antique furniture shop.

Journalism has a long and honorable history in Indonesia, beginning with the final decades of Dutch rule. The Dutch, who had colonized or otherwise commercially dominated the archipelago since the seventeenth century, had suffered a nationwide crisis of conscience following exposés of oppression, brutality and disenfranchisement in their "model" colony in the late nineteenth century. By the early years of the twentieth century, what was known as the "ethical policy," forced on the colonial administration by the government in Holland, had created a coterie of pribumi elite educated in Dutch high schools and professional colleges such as the STOVIA, which produced hundreds of para-medical practitioners. For the first time in history, relatively small but nonetheless significant numbers of pribumi had exposure to Western political philosophy and access to anti-colonial or revolutionary literature widely available in Dutch. This nascent pribumi intelligentsia, along with other organizations formed along social or religious lines, conspired to launch Indonesia's first anti-colonial movement aimed at moving forward into nationhood rather than retreating into a misty feudal past.

During the decades before the Second World War, the nationalists established several newspapers and other publications promoting their cause, pushing the tolerance of the colonial administration to the limit. The Dutch were initially reluctant to violate their own cultural heritage of a free and responsible press to clamp down on the new publications. The best of them denied the government a good cause to attack by filling their pages with accurate reporting, informed opinion, and, since most contributors were educated Javanese, polite, restrained language. It was activist journalism of a high order.

Nevertheless, the nationalists eventually pushed the Dutch too far. By 1942, when the Japanese invaded the archipelago, most nationalist newspapers had been closed down and the contributors exiled or imprisoned. Journalism lay dormant during the occupation as the press was placed under Japanese control and used only for propaganda.

In August 1945, during the power vacuum between the Japanese surrender and the arrival of British mopping-up forces, the charismatic Soekarno, who had emerged as the most visible figure of the nationalist movement, declared the Republic of Indonesia an independent nation. After an uneasy co-existence and several violent incidents, the Dutch moved to crush the new government. Soekarno and the other Founding Fathers retreated to Yogyakarta, one of the twin centers of Javanese culture and society, where they were joined by a motley mix of populist firebrands and militia forces to fight a fierce four-year battle to keep their new nation in existence.

In Yogyakarta Pak Trisno had his first taste of journalism. Usmar Ismail, later to become a pioneering filmmaker, published the Patriot, a newspaper whose primary mission was to sustain morale as nationalist leaders lobbied world governments for recognition of their infant republic. Pak Trisno roamed the city and countryside, reporting on the suffering and resilience of a people fighting for their independence.

The Republic of Indonesia's survival was assured in the last days of 1949, when the Dutch capitulated under international diplomatic pressure and recognized the new government. As the heady days of revolutionary fervor gave way to the harsh realities of nation-building, Indonesia staggered into the post-colonial era singularly ill-equipped for nationhood. With an economy ravaged by almost a decade of wartime occupation and post-war revolution, the infant nation made little headway against poverty, illiteracy, and disease.

Nevertheless, scores of newspapers and other publications appeared. In 1951, Pak Trisno traveled to Europe on a Dutch "colonial-guilt" scholarship program for promising young Indonesians. Returning from Holland in 1952 with the rudiments of European liberal philosophy, and fired with humanitarian fervor, Pak Trisno plunged into advocacy journalism, documenting the plight of the common people as a half-made, fractious republic lurched from one crisis to the next.

By the mid-sixties, Indonesia was in a state of national paralysis as competing factions vied for supremacy. The situation came to a head during the early evening of 30 September 1965. The sequence of events during that evening and the following days are open to a multitude of interpretations. The only events subject to objective confirmation are the kidnapping of several generals—and a lieutenant by mistake—and the military occupation of Merdeka Square.

In the aftermath, a previously obscure general named Soeharto (Javanese often have only one name) emerged as de facto commander of the armed forces and eventually the nation. In origin, mannerism, and style the exact opposite of his flamboyant and sophisticated predecessor, Soeharto patiently consolidated his own position and maneuvered Soekarno out of power.

During those months, the nation was convulsed by an orgy of violence seldom matched in modern times. The new government blamed the PKI, Indonesia's three-million-member communist party, for the murder of the army officers. To eliminate the PKI, the Indonesian people—abetted by the military—executed between five hundred thousand and one million of their compatriots. Card-carrying communists accounted for a minority of victims. Creditors, owners of prime farming land, rival suitors, and anyone with an unresolved feud were branded communist traitors and summarily executed.

Other victims were condemned though association with PKI-sponsored organizations or even, as in Pak Trisno's case, artistic or literary style. Though never matching the flowery rhetoric of his colleagues, whose articles in mainstream publications had the flavor of diatribes scribbled in seedy cafes by caffeine-crazed revolutionaries, Pak Trisno liberally quoted Marx and other socialist luminaries in his articles. Pak Trisno was arrested a few weeks after the army officer killings and placed in Group B, which included ambassadors, cabinet ministers, and journalists. All were accused of subversion, none ever saw the inside of a courtroom, yet most spent many years in jail.

Pak Trisno described his years in prison as more of an inconvenience than a hardship. He was spared transfer to the penal colony on Buru Island, instead being shuffled from one prison to another in Jakarta and environs. As an educated man, he was highly respected by other prisoners, particularly the common, non-political inmates, who often asked for help writing

letters to family and to others who might help secure
their release. For the most part, the prison authorities
were benevolent, allowing Pak Trisno and other Group
B prisoners to transform their bare cells into Spartan
but comfortable homes. Pak Trisno had lost his library
when arresting officers ransacked his house and carted
off his possessions, but managed by trading favors to
build a modest book collection, though restricted to
fiction and non-political subjects.

By the mid-seventies, the New Order was in firm
control of Indonesia. Along with many other political
prisoners, Pak Trisno was released in 1974. He was now
alone. His wife had divorced him and remarried—with
unseemly haste—soon after his imprisonment. His
other surviving relatives lived in distant East Java.

Pak Trisno had always chosen his friends wisely.
Many of his colleagues from the glory days were willing
to risk official displeasure by helping Pak Trisno
survive. In 1980, a friend who had achieved great
success in the booming oil business loaned Pak Trisno
enough cash to open a modest antique shop—
neglecting to ask for repayment. With the assistance
of family and friends in East and Central Java, Pak
Trisno sought out antique furniture and quality
reproductions to sell to the foreigners now flocking to
Indonesia.

Pak Trisno's shop lies close to the expat enclaves
in South Jakarta, which expanded throughout the
eighties as a shortage of local managerial and technical
expertise created a huge demand for expatriates in the
growing economy. Most of Pak Trisno's customers were
foreigners, which suited him just fine. He dealt only
reluctantly with the OKB, *orang kaya baru* or *nouveau
riche* Indonesians, many of whom did not seem to

appreciate the fine workmanship of Pak Trisno's carefully selected collection. Retreating into a mystic Islam heavily laced with Javanese philosophy, Pak Trisno lived modestly and quietly until Krismon, when the plunging rupiah made Indonesian furniture the best deal in the world.

With his fluent Dutch and English, Pak Trisno became a favored supplier for bargain-hunting furniture buyers. Most Western buyers went directly to the provincial factories or home industries, browbeating the owners into giving the lowest possible prices. The buyers then had to deal with endless delivery and quality problems. Pak Trisno's customers gladly paid premium prices in return for ironclad guarantees of delivery and quality, backed up through his long-standing relationships with furniture makers.

With trusted buyers scouring the island for antiques or supervising the manufacture of quality reproductions in home industries along Java's North Coast, Pak Trisno spent his days in friendly negotiation with buyers or cultivating the traditional interests of a Javanese aristocrat. Smiling to show I was in jest, as I did not want to offend the old gentleman, I asked how he felt now that he was an OKB.

Pak Trisno played along, telling me he was not an OKB, but a KKK.

"Ku Klux Klan?" I asked, puzzled at this unfamiliar acronym.

"*Kaya Karena Krismon*," Pak Trisno replied. Rich because of the economic crisis.

Kambing Putih

TRISAKTI UNIVERSITY'S COMMERCIAL-AREA location reflects the mission of the institution and primary concerns of the faculty and student body. Where the state-run University of Indonesia trains the nation's future academics and bureaucrats in a tranquil suburban campus at Jakarta's southern perimeter, Trisakti churns out the professionals needed to run the nuts and bolts of the economy. Ten years ago the Indonesian government moved the University of Indonesia to the current isolated location to discourage student involvement in politics. Even if the government could have coerced privately owned Trisakti to relocate, I doubt they would have bothered. Like the passengers of the sleek BMW sedans and drivers of boxy delivery trucks fighting their way across the complicated intersection adjacent to the campus, Trisakti students, sole concern was to reach their destination and make some money. Such single-minded devotion leaves little time for politics.

The economic and political chaos during the months after the Trisakti shootings were not sufficient to distract attention from assignments and exams. Even the four martyred students receded into dim memory, as though they had left the university through graduation rather than being gunned down in the parking lot.

Monica, however, was having difficulty returning to the student grind. She went through the motions, attending classes and working on assignments, without being able to concentrate fully on her studies. Her academic career took an unexpected turn one day, when she showed her MPR photographs to a group of classmates during a break. The group included a classmate's boyfriend, Ronny, who was studying commercial art. Ronny praised the photos, complimenting Monica on her sense of composition. Monica blushed, attributing the good image quality to the automatic features of the expensive camera "Uncle" Liem had given her.

Ronny disagreed. "A camera does not take pictures by itself," he said. "A person not blessed with a photographer's eye can only produce a mediocre image, though it might have perfect focus and exposure."

Ronny suggested that Monica visit the graphic arts faculty, perhaps to take courses or arrange for private instruction. That was how Monica came to join the university's photography club; Ronny's recommendation gained her immediate entry. Actually, the others seemed to be happy the club finally had a Chinese member. They appointed Monica treasurer, in the belief that only an ethnic Chinese person would be strict enough to make members pay their dues and manage the accounts.

During that time I visited Trisakti at least once a week. Monica and I met in the small lounge outside the video editing suite, set up for students to sneak a quick cigarette and coffee, neither being allowed inside the suite itself. She looked out of place, sporting the well-groomed look of a business major rather than the studied scruffiness preferred by graphic arts students.

I asked her what life was like for a Chinese student two months after the May Riots.

"Everyone is nice to me," Monica said, "Pribumi students who had hardly noticed me before are so friendly, even phoning me at home to see if I am okay."

Monica felt much of this concern was over-reaction, people bending over backward to prove that they, too, were appalled by the events surrounding the May Riots. I met Monica frequently during subsequent weeks. She always seemed to have time to talk. I wondered if she was lonely, as many of her acquaintances were moving to presumably safer homes in Singapore, Australia, and North America.

Monica often showed me the photos she was taking for her on-going self-documentation project. Like a sensible novice writer who sticks to familiar subjects, Monica photographed her family environment and daily routine, which were now undergoing strange adjustments because of the tense and unstable situation. One quietly evocative image showed Monica's mother and grandmother standing in front of a kitchen cupboard bursting with enough rice and packaged noodles to last for weeks. Monica mentioned her kitchen now looked like the Malang dry-goods shop where she had grown up, which led her to telling me her family history.

Monica's family emigrated to Indonesia from southern China during the early 1930s. After several years as a warehouse clerk in Surabaya, her grandfather took advantage of the extensive mutual support facilities provided by Chinese clan associations to set up a dry-goods shop in an East Java village. He soon became the village's unofficial banker, the lender of first and last resort. Villagers would pledge their crops in return for cash, often to pay for weddings or other ceremonial occasions.

The Japanese conquest of the Dutch East Indies in early 1942 shattered this quiet, ordered life. Though the Japanese despised the Chinese, Monica's family were spared internment, the fate of those Europeans not able to evacuate in time. Monica's grandparents endured wartime hardships until August 1945, when the Japanese surrendered and, in far-off Jakarta, Soekarno declared the birth of the Republic of Indonesia.

The end of the war brought little respite. Four years of shipping blockades and disruption of internal transportation resulting from the fighting between militant nationalists and returning Dutch colonialists simply exacerbated wartime hardships. Only when the Dutch finally accepted the independence of their former colony in December 1949 did Monica's grandparents rebuild their business, hoping to live peacefully and profitably in the new Republic of Indonesia.

In the beginning the future looked bright for small-scale businessmen like Monica's grandfather. Stepping into the oversize shoes of the Dutch, pribumi Indonesians used their Chinese compatriots to reestablish distribution networks and begin the long-overdue process of industrial development. With the Dutch gone, the military and pribumi elite became the nation's new overseers, while ethnic Chinese residents remained the distributors and traders, factory owners, shopkeepers, moneylenders and, whenever required, scapegoats, or *kambing putih*—a play with the Indonesian phrase *kambing hitam*.

The first setback for Chinese Indonesians came in 1956, when the government moved to empower indigenous entrepreneurs by barring ethnic Chinese from village-level trade. Monica's grandparents moved to Malang, a pleasant, thriving town in the East Java highlands. Using their own savings supplemented with clan association loans, they set up a successful dry-goods distribution business, prospering and raising a family until the next great trial for Chinese Indonesians, the anti-Communist pogroms in the wake of the New Order government's consolidation of power.

Though many of the massacres of supposed Communists during the mid-sixties occurred in East Java, relatively few Chinese Indonesians were victims. Emerging unscathed from that tumultuous period, Monica's family continued to flourish as East Java emerged from rural poverty to comparative prosperity with coffee plantations in the south and a thriving industrial area around Surabaya on the coast. The dry-goods shop earned enough to send Monica's father to university in Surabaya, where he graduated with a degree in Mechanical Engineering—and acquired a wife.

Monica spent a pleasant childhood in Malang, though most residents of that provincial highland town harbored considerable resentment toward the pale-skinned, predominantly Christian Chinese people who dominated the local economy. When she was old enough to understand, Monica's parents taught her about the "cold war" between ethnic Chinese and pribumi Indonesians, the constant background of tension Monica could almost feel and see, like a miasma of envy and contempt polluting the crisp mountain air.

Monica's family moved to Jakarta in the late eighties, where her father built a successful practice as a construction engineer. The soaring, glass-faced towers Monica's father helped build were an appropriate metaphor for the way the Indonesian economy operated during the Soeharto era. In building the New Order Mega Block, Chinese and pribumi professionals installed the air-conditioning, lights, and other essential building components, while a tiny coterie of trusted ethnic Chinese businessmen raised the offshore loans to provide the financing and operated the machinery of corruption needed to extract permits from the thicket of contradictory civic and national regulations.

Common Indonesians flocked from the countryside to carry out the backbreaking work of construction, foreign consultants earned every dollar of their exorbitant salaries ensuring schedules were kept and specifications met, while the military, in this case civilian security forces hired to safeguard the project against street criminals, spent most of their time forcing farmers to sell their land to developers for derisory sums and collecting protection money from the food stalls and other small businesses springing up around any construction project. The system operated so well, and created such impressive results, few noticed the metaphorical edifice had been erected on wholly inadequate foundations. Even a minor earth tremor would bring the whole structure crashing down.

When the East Asian economic earthquake toppled the New Order Mega Block, Chinese Indonesians assumed their traditional role of scapegoats. Food riots hit many Indonesian towns in the last weeks of 1997. There was a hiatus during the fasting month of Ramadan, then in February 1998 mob violence struck in East Java. Street gangs looted the dry-goods shop in Malang, former customers carting away sacks of rice while Monica's grandparents cowered in a barricaded back room. Monica's father immediately flew to Malang, helped his parents clean up the damage, and brought his mother to Jakarta. The "cold war" had once again turned hot.

By August, Monica's self-documentation project included several shots of friends and acquaintances in tearful farewells. Her circle of friends was shrinking fast as many of Jakarta's Chinese community emigrated to Australia or North America. Monica had spent much of her free time at tropical Indonesia's only ice-skating rink, set up in a large shopping mall in a predominantly Chinese area of Jakarta. In the months following the May Riots most members of her ice-skating team moved, appropriately enough, to Canada. For many, the move was traumatic. Monica's friends told her of selling every possession to scrape up airfares, arriving with nothing, willing to accept any employment. Letters Monica received weeks later told of parents and siblings—graduate students, professionals and businessmen—washing dishes, sweeping streets, working punishing hours for meager pay to gain a precarious foothold in their new home.

I asked Monica if any of her friends returned to China.

"No way," she said. "The Chinese people think we are foreigners, no better than white people."

Life was no easier for those electing—or compelled —to stay behind. I accompanied Monica on a trip to

Glodok, which I had not visited since the riots. Though the smashed windows and gutted shops offered eloquent evidence of the unrest three months before, the street was alive with activity. Many looted shops had been refurbished and restocked, other vendors had set up makeshift stalls in front of the burnt buildings.

On the other hand, Monica's photographs of a housing estate in West Jakarta, where a distant relative of Monica's mother owned a house, depicted less a suburban idyll than a pioneer settlement in hostile territory. Concrete barricades restricted traffic through the main gate, perimeter walls sported shining coils of barbed wire, and armed guards patrolled empty streets.

In one photograph, a housewife smiled in embarrassment as she awkwardly held the *parang* her husband kept atop the bedroom wardrobe cabinet. I had a fleeting, quickly suppressed thought that the knife was intended to use on herself and her daughter as much as for a futile show of defense against home invaders. Three months after the riots, reports were emerging of severe mental disturbance and suicides among rape victims. While the government and military continued to deny any occurrences of systematic sexual assault, the Chinese community knew the reports were horribly real. Several of Monica's photographs conveyed an almost palpable sense of dread.

A visit to "Uncle" Liem's *krupuk* factory brought the viewers into another world. In a series of awkwardly staged shots, Liem is shown distributing packages of essential food items to his employees with a paternal air, as the recipients bow in gratitude. Monica told me she had wanted a shot of Liem

screaming abuse at a shop foreman, a frequent
occurrence, but the wily factory owner was on his best
behavior for his favorite "niece's" visit. She also wanted
a shot of Liem and his partners speaking in Chinese
at a business meeting with pribumi managers, but did
not know how to convey the concept in still images.

"Why would you want to show that?" I asked.

"Because it's what I hate most about Jakarta
Chinese people. They talk in Chinese so no one else
can understand."

"Not even you?"

"Not a word."

"That's probably because many Chinese people in
Jakarta speak a different dialect than those from East
Java. Which dialect do your grandparents speak?"

"Dialect?" Monica asked.

"Yeah," I said, "Hokkien, or Hakka, or what?"

As Monica frowned in puzzlement I realized she
did not know the "Chinese language" was comprised
of many mutually unintelligible spoken dialects,
though the written ideograms are identical and
understandable by all. I had the impression that
despite her East Asian features and ability to manage
money, this young woman was no more Chinese than I.

As Monica concentrated on photographing
Jakarta's Chinese Indonesians at the grass-roots level,
showing them cowering behind concrete walls or
valiantly rebuilding their lives, a debate on the
"Chinese Question" raged in the media and other
public forums. Actually, the word debate, with its
connotations of structured argument and intellectual
rigor, is too generous a description; "mindless polemic"
is more accurate.

In newspaper opinion pages presumably educated and worldly correspondents abandoned reason, perspective, and fairness, letting fly unsubstantiated generalities and dubious assertions. Balanced argument, when it existed, was overwhelmed by an onslaught of grotesque cartoon images: terrified schoolgirls in torn uniforms menaced by a muscular, crew-cut hoodlums with shiny boots and pants at half-mast; slit-eyed Shylocks dividing corruption spoils with Soeharto-gang scoundrels.

The Chinese Question was a frequent topic of conversation with Pak Trisno. During one discussion of the supposed Chinese dominance of the Indonesian economy, Pak Trisno told me a slightly derogatory joke he had heard from an expatriate customer some years before. Unless he was completely insensitive, the foreigner presumably had forgotten he was in the company of an Indonesian, as I often did when conversing in English with Pak Trisno. The joke asks how many Javanese are needed to change a light bulb. The answer is three: one to serve tea, one to get the required permits from the government, and the third to run out and find a Chinese who knows how to do it.

I laughed, and tried to remember of a similar joke I had once heard about Balinese and burnt-out light bulbs that I could tell him in return. But Pak Trisno was not finished. In the style of many Javanese mystics, he was using humor to make a serious point.

"Most foreigners would think the joke means pribumi Indonesians are lazy. That is not true at all."

I nodded in agreement. During my years working with seismic survey crews in the Kalimantan oil fields, or exploring remote corners of Java and Sumatra on my trail bike, I had seen terraced fields carved into mountain slopes and much other evidence of prodigious industry. Driving past rice fields, I often wondered how long I would last planting, weeding, or harvesting in the hot sun.

"In fact, all three Javanese are busy," Pak Trisno said, "but Westerners do not think they are being productive."

"You have to admit, serving tea and hanging around a government office hardly gets the job done," I replied, wondering why we were analyzing a silly light-bulb joke to death.

Pak Trisno ducked his head slightly and looked at me over the top rim of his reading glasses, his way of showing mild exasperation.

"You miss the point. Observing proper etiquette and following correct procedures are central to our way of life. We feel the details are best left to others."

"But if the Chinese guy changes all the light bulbs in town," I replied, getting into the spirit of the conversation, "he will eventually control the light bulb business."

"Certainly so. But the pribumi have the final say. We can always choose to live in darkness."

Down and Out in Kemang

SPENDING MY EVENINGS WITH NEWLY IMPOVERISHED Indoyups at Kafé Tirtayasa, I effectively dropped out of the expatriate social scene. After a few weeks my expat friends—who all enjoyed dollar incomes—complained I had vanished. When several insisted on treating me to drinks or dinner at one of the usual haunts I embarked on a new career. I became a professional guest.

I quickly gained considerable proficiency in reaching for my wallet at the exact moment to show a willingness to contribute money while minimizing the risk I would actually have to pay for a meal whose cost amounted to a large portion of my weekly food budget.

I was probably wasting my effort. I doubt if anyone begrudged, or even noticed, my involuntary freeloading. They were too busy fighting for the privilege of picking up the check, treating their friends to drinks and meals for no more than pocket change.

Such free-spending foreigners were termed DIA, Dollar-Income Assholes. Many DIAs were not intentionally obnoxious, just insensitive. I had to implore several friends not to use the term "dirt-cheap" in conjunction with rupiah figures containing more than four zeros.

Expats and other foreigners were not the only DIAs in town. The plunging rupiah had slashed raw material and labor costs for almost all Indonesian export commodities. Indonesians operating their own businesses in resource extraction, agribusiness, fisheries, or export-oriented manufacturing saw the rupiah value of their revenue multiply overnight.

"Where is Krismon?" became a favorite topic of conversation. While the local and international media presented distressing stories of abject suffering and gloomy predictions of impending economic disaster, life on the streets and restaurants seemed unchanged. I wondered what someone parachuted into Indonesia with no knowledge of recent events would make of the situation. During my years in the oil fields, I had heard numerous stories of oil workers who had taken a head start on leave-time carousing disembarking from the company jet at the wrong airport. I imagined the reaction of one such roughneck, new to the region, who was too inebriated to notice the "Welcome to Indonesia" sign in the arrival hall.

He probably would not realize he had arrived in a nation suffering the deepest economic crisis in a generation. On the drive from the airport he would see no outward signs of distress, at least, nothing qualitatively different from the beggars and other signs of wretched poverty seen in most developing countries. He might notice the eerie quiet in his almost-empty hotel, but a short ride in a brand-new taxi to a trendy nightspot would dispel any doubts he was anywhere but in a booming metropolis.

As he pushed his way to the bar though a crowd of affluent foreigners and Indonesians he might overhear boasts of luxury automobiles, yachts, and country villas bought at fire-sale prices. He might become dimly aware of impending disaster if he stumbled into a group of World Bank or International Monetary Fund consultants discussing the moribund banking industry over premium whiskey and twenty-dollar cigars. Even if our hypothetical roughneck understood the conversation, he would brush it off as alarmist nonsense. Even on the Titanic, they stopped partying only immediately after hitting the iceberg.

For the majority of Indonesians, however, life was no party. Essential items such as rice, cooking oil, and onions shot up in price as supply lines were broken and products diverted to the far-more-lucrative export market. The poorest folk restricted themselves to one meal a day, and many abandoned rice for cheaper cassava and other less nutritious foods. For some, it was not much of a change. They cut down again on their already meager diet, and cinched their belts another notch, often living off the land, even in the cities.

For me, hunkering down was not an option. My relative poverty put me in the unenviable category of *bule kere*, a Javanese term loosely translated as "white trash," with the same connotations of moral disapproval. I was a walking oxymoron, like jumbo shrimp or military intelligence.

Though there were impoverished Dutch and other Europeans during colonial times, since Independence the only white foreigners most Indonesians encountered were technical experts or tourists. Even the restricted budgets of anthropologists and other academics undertaking long-term research programs provide a standard of living most Indonesians can only dream about. Excepted are priests and missionaries, who eschew material wealth for spiritual reasons, and the volunteer development workers, usually students or retirees, who assist community-based programs for no remuneration beyond accommodation expenses and pocket money. As practices involving self-denial and community service are common in many Indonesian cultures, such foreigners are welcomed and often highly respected. For other foreigners, poverty is regarded as an affront against nature, disturbing the harmonious order of the universe.

Fortunately, in Indonesia, as in much of Asia, appearances are everything. If I could not be a standard-issue affluent expatriate, I could at least live like one. Ironically, Krismon provided me with that opportunity.

When the plunging exchange rate made dollar-based compensation packages prohibitively expensive, large numbers of foreign managers and technical consultants were shown the door—often with unseemly haste, leaving whole blocks of elite-district residences vacant with no prospective tenants in sight. Several weeks after the May Riots, a friend then living in California contacted me to say his house—more accurately his wife's house—was unoccupied. He asked me, if it would not be too much trouble, to move into his house and take care of it. My only responsibilities would be to pay staff salaries and utility bills.

It was a dream deal. After months in a cramped and noisy rented room, I found myself lord and master of a roomy villa occupying a lush quarter-hectare deep in the expatriate enclave of Kemang.

A country suburb now engulfed by the city, large houses and spacious lots made Kemang a preferred area for expatriates. Rents are quoted in dollars, payable at least two years in advance. Late-model Harley Davidson motorcycles roar along the street, sport utility vehicles jockey for parking space in front of trendy restaurants and cafés. Step into Kemchicks, a supermarket founded by a Kemang native who once sold chicken eggs door-to-door from a bicycle, and the heat, noise and squalor of Jakarta fades away, the atmosphere and clientele similar to a specialty foods store in an up-market European or American neighborhood.

Kemang's almost total isolation from mainstream Jakarta spawned a number of legends, such as the belief expat wives bathe only in bottled water and spend the day lazing around the pool drinking gin tonics. While stories of hygienic paranoia and extravagant consumption among expatriates were exaggerations— in most cases—the intensive socializing was not. One old Kemang hand described life in his neighborhood as first-year college with money. The relative freedom from financial worry, constant round of social events, and new horizons for sexual activity all evoked young adulthood, not mid-life stability.

Every weekend, word would circulate of an open-house party, often with a map showing the path down tortuous back streets. Map or no, the party was never hard to find. A hundred meters away, security guards would be directing traffic and assigning parking spaces. A live band, a hired DJ, or the host's two-thousand-strong collection of pirated CDs and tapes provided the music, a sponsoring company the beer, and that season's crop of teenage party girls the atmosphere and after-hours entertainment.

That world disappeared with the expat exodus, replaced by more subdued gatherings among die-hard survivors. Raucous, high-living Kemang was once again a quiet suburb. Around my house, quiet was an understatement. The house was one of six situated on a cul-de-sac. The other houses, built as investments to rent to expats, were now empty, a Spanish-Med ghost town.

I welcomed the isolation and freedom from distraction. I converted one bedroom into an office and settled down to concentrate on my work, insulated from frenetic Jakarta, and, more importantly, free from the struggle to come up with the rent every month. Then I discovered the minimum utility rate.

The house was wired for three air conditioners, two water heaters, and external floodlights—33,000 watts in all. Though I deactivated the air conditioners, set the water heaters to tepid, and substituted the floods with an industrial-strength flashlight, I still had to pay a set monthly rate. I tried to have the wattage reduced, which would drop me into a lower rate bracket, but this required the signature of the homeowner, legally my friend's Indonesian wife. She refused, knowing they would have to pay a huge amount to increase the wattage again to accommodate future paying tenants.

I could not even draw up a monthly budget. During the later Soeharto years, when corruption and collusive business practices grew unchecked, the government had coerced the PLN, the national electricity utility, into disadvantageous agreements with foreign companies and their local partners to build and operate new power generators. As the local partners were all First Family members or cronies, electricity the utility did not really need was purchased with dollars at rates that only made sense if the economy had continued its five-to-seven percent annual growth rate.

As the economy plunged, utility bills soared. In all, my free ride was costing me more than twice as much as my previous rented room. My options for reducing monthly costs boiled down to the standard fixtures of every Kemang residence: the backyard swimming pool and the household staff.

I weighed my alternatives for the swimming pool. I could not ignore it, as turning off the filter would only convert the pool into an olive-green mosquito farm. I could not afford to hire a water truck to suction up the contents, and with the piping clogged from lack of maintenance, opening the drain valve would only create a suburban wetland in my downhill neighbor's back yard.

I considered the household staff. An unwritten rule mandates that every expatriate Kemang household must employ at least three servants: a maid, a gardener, and a night watchman.

Releasing the night watchman, who is usually a former policemen or soldier, is asking for trouble, if not from criminals then from the ex-employee himself. With four bedrooms and almost five hundred square meters of common living space to clean and dust I did not consider letting go of the maid.

That left Pak Tatang, the gardener. Pak Tatang was the Indonesian equivalent of an old family retainer. My friend had inherited him when he bought the house. His only duties, it seemed, were to weed the garden and vacuum leaves off the pool. When I suggested he take early retirement, Pak Tatang was willing, as long as I paid a sizable bonus based on his years of service. Protestations that I had no responsibility for his previous employment fell on deaf ears. Like an heirloom no one wants but cannot sell or throw away, Pak Tatang had landed in my lap.

As I pondered a compromise I might reach with the old man, I learned that Pak Tatang's three hundred thousand rupiah monthly salary was the only regular cash income of his village in Southwest Java. This region had been hard hit by Krismon as many families relied almost entirely on the support of spouses and children working in cities and industrial estates throughout West Java. With the massive layoffs still continuing, life in these villages was desperate. International humanitarian aid agencies warned of malnutrition physically and intellectually stunting a generation of children.

If I let Pak Tatang go, word would circulate around the neighborhood I had fired a nice old man and starved his home village so I would not have to drain the swimming pool.

"*Dasar bule*," the neighbors would say, painting a verbal portrait of me enjoying a poolside beer while Pak Tatang's grandchildren whimpered in hunger. "Isn't it just like a white man."

Psychologists say the common dream of being naked in a public place is a subconscious warning that you cannot live up to your billing. I started having these dreams a couple of weeks after moving into the Kemang Palace, portending an embarrassing revelation of my true situation.

One evening, as I partied with some friends at the Hard Rock Café, practicing the slow draw on my wallet, a former business colleague approached my table with a young Indonesian couple in tow. Ever the hustler, he insisted on buying me another drink in the hopes I would pass along the telephone numbers of contacts in the advertising and television industry. Quickly tiring of his conversation but not wanting to be rude, I turned my attention to his friends, Erik and Siti.

While in many western cultures single men and women often maintain close friendships without being romantically involved, in Indonesia, a young, unmarried couple claiming to be "just friends" are regarded as merely being discreet about their affair. However, after a few minutes conversing with Erik and Siti, I gained the strong impression they were indeed no more than good friends.

I was one of the few to believe them. Among the skeptics was a girl sitting with friends at another table, whom Erik had recently met. As a favor, Siti asked me to play the role of her boyfriend for the girl's benefit. To complete the deception, I had to escort Siti out of the café, leaving Erik behind.

Since Siti lived in a suburb adjacent to Kemang, I had intended to act the consummate gentleman by escorting her to her front door. However, several beers followed by twenty minutes in the back seat of a taxi with a beautiful woman can foil the best-laid plans. As we shared a late breakfast on the Kemang Palace back terrace the following morning, Siti complimented me on the house and asked how much rent I paid, an inquiry not considered impolite in Indonesia. Carried away by the occasion, I was reluctant to admit my status as glorified caretaker. Instead, I mumbled something about the steep drop in house rents in response to Krismon. She regarded the terrace and adjoining living room, filled with comfortable rattan and reproduction antique furnishings, with an approving eye. She murmured: "I could live here," then gave me a coy glance over her cup as she sipped her coffee.

Later that day I told Farid that I was worried my precarious finances disqualified me from any relationship. Although, as one nice girl said: "Love isn't just about money, you know," I was all-too-aware that when the economic crunch came, as it must considering by irregular income, the relationship would probably suffer irreparable damage.

I could not even nip the affair in the bud. If I tried to discourage Siti by admitting my true financial situation, she would be highly insulted, believing I considered her a *cewek matre*, a material girl. Inventing some excuse or simply not calling her would only reinforce the widely held and largely accurate perception that bules are jerks.

When I asked Farid for advice, he only shook his head in exasperation.

"Jakarta is one of the easiest places in the world to get laid," he reminded me, "and you turn it into an existential dilemma."

Though Siti greatly enhanced the atmosphere of the Kemang Palace, her continued residence only compounded my financial problems. When we went out together, Siti insisted we call a taxi, as she was concerned about possible disparaging comments from other passengers if we took public transportation. Most of her telephone calls seemed to be to cell phones, racking up huge airtime charges.

When I mentioned that we had to cut down

expenses, Siti, ever practical, had another suggestion. Considering we were using less than half of the available living space, I should set up a *bule indekos*, a rooming house for foreigners who could pay enough dollar-denominated rent each month to cover utilities and staff payments.

I thought it over and decided to follow her advice. I placed an advertisement in *The Jakarta Post* classifieds. After running the ad for a week I received only one serious call, from a recently arrived freelance journalist looking for a quiet place to write. The thought of two writers sharing a house reminded me of the Chinese ideogram depicting two wives under one roof, which signifies unqualified disaster.

The day after giving up on the *bule indekos* idea I happened to e-mail one of the first friends I made in Indonesia. An academic specializing in Javanese performing arts, especially the *gamelan*, the bronze-gong orchestra which provides the musical accompaniment for most types of traditional performances, Adam had moved back to the United States in the mid-eighties, when his grant money ran out. After trading sporadic letters for a few years, we lost touch. Needing some background research on Javanese music for a web site project, I tracked down his e-mail address through another Javanist and sent him a message, asking, among other things, where in the world he was.

The answer was "five blocks away." The drastic devaluation of the rupiah had made his long-planned sabbatical year in Indonesia possible. He had arrived three weeks before and was now wearing out his welcome at a succession of friends' houses. At my suggestion, he moved into the Kemang Palace the following day: lock, stock, and gamelan.

Siti did make herself useful in one respect. Pak Tatang liked to pass time chatting or playing cards with his colleagues who looked after the other empty houses on the block. When required, Siti can emit a high-pitched, penetrating shout. Whenever Pak Tatang went missing, she would call out from the second-story balcony. Pak Tatang would emerge from one of the houses and reluctantly saunter back to see what duties awaited him.

I kid her that her voice is useful for calling across the rice fields, which annoys her no end. Born in Jakarta, Siti considers herself an urban Indonesian, and takes grave offense when she is compared to her village brethren.

Town and Country

T HE PROMINENT ROLE OF A YOUNG ARISTOCRAT in a
nineteenth-century Hungarian rebellion against
deeply entrenched feudal privilege led contemporary
observers to remark: "Hungarians cannot even manage
a revolution without a count." A century-and-a-half
later, with Indonesia's reform movement in disarray,
President Habibie's surprise moves to implement a
reform agenda seemed to indicate only the New Order
government could organize its own replacement.

Starting with the announcement of his new cabinet
two days after his inauguration, the Habibie
administration set a style diametrically opposed to the
taciturn formality of the Soeharto years. I had not been
able to suppress a grin when Habibie announced his
cabinet line-up, his voice steadily rising in pitch as
he named cabinet appointees replete with the string
of academic titles beloved by Indonesians. Each
repetition of "Professor Doctor..." confirmed a break
from the almost willful lack of competence of later New
Order cabinets, when technical or managerial ability
stood distant second to blind loyalty to the old man
as the prerequisite qualification.

I was also impressed to see the game new president
deal amiably with interruptions during speeches—
unimaginable in Soeharto's time—and bantering with

an increasingly aggressive press, to the horror of palace bureaucrats, who were afraid he might blurt out something of real substance. I doubt if they were any less disapproving of their new president's penchant for belting out karaoke tunes at formal receptions.

Habibie's spontaneous style baffled and amused foreign journalists. Expressive to the point of caricature—one reporter described him as "Elmer Fudd on Speed"—and throwing out ideas as often half-baked as fully thought out, he was charitably regarded as a nutcase. They made light of Habibie's nebulous management style, citing a litany of organizational missteps—unrecorded official conversations, cell phones deactivated for late payments—as though they were hallmarks of a singularly inept presidency instead of the routine screw-ups found in any Indonesian organization.

I met Habibie in 1986, several years after Soeharto had asked him to leave Germany, where he had been educated and subsequently had become a leading aviation engineer, and return to his homeland as Indonesia's Minister of Technology. In his new position, Habibie set about to transform the nation's fledgling aviation industry, which previously had concentrated on developing rugged, easy-to-maintain aircraft to provide much-needed transportation links between remote communities. Habibie's grand vision was to transplant advanced manufacturing facilities and resources to Indonesia—like a pre-fabricated luxury vacation house erected on a remote mountain top—in order to stimulate the development of locally based high-technology industries.

I was dragged to his spacious ministerial office and put on display as the token foreigner in some dubious advertising project connected with Indonesian aviation. Sitting with Habibie at a huge table filled with model airplanes of every description, I was reminded of a friend describing Habibie as "the world's oldest kid with the world's biggest toy." Now he had an entire nation to play with, and no father figure to slap him down if he misbehaved.

If journalists dismissed Habibie as a clown or New Order stooge, the business community had a more positive view. The previous January, the currency market had reflected the general dismay at Soeharto's anointment of the unpredictable, free-spending technocrat as Indonesia's next Vice President by plunging to a record low of 17,000 against the American dollar. Three months into Habibie's presidency, many business people and economic observers began to see hope in the new government, especially after the rupiah began a dramatic revaluation, at one point approaching 7,000 rupiah to the dollar.

Spending at least one afternoon each week on Pak Trisno's back terrace, an oasis of calm and rationality amid the growing chaos, we often discussed Habibie and his efforts to form an effective government. Pak Trisno admitted that Habibie's predisposition for firing off concepts and solutions in all directions like a fire hose released from the fireman's grasp defied any attempt at rational policy making. But he wondered if anyone could be effective in Habibie's position. The new cabinet of academics and Soeharto holdovers trying to maintain a precarious footing amid social and economic chaos had little chance of initiating, much less implementing, any form of coherent policy.

Pak Trisno believed history might show Habibie

had been uniquely suited to fill the president's chair during the transition time—the "Odd Man In," as one international newsmagazine called him. Though corruption remained rampant and many observers believed any economic improvement was more the result of outside factors than action taken by the Habibie administration, he had made significant symbolic gestures, such as releasing political prisoners and freeing the press from oppressive censorship.

"Perhaps his weaknesses are actually his strengths," Pak Trisno said. "By appearing informal and firing off crackpot ideas, Habibie is demystifying the presidency, the first step in creating a more open political system."

If Habibie's contribution to the resurgence of open political dialog is subject to debate, there is no doubt he was the primary impetus for the second round of student demonstrations beginning in late September. Notwithstanding the Habibie government's initiatives to correct the abuses of the previous government, the students were unable to believe Habibie, whose close relationship to the former president generated vicious rumors he was Soeharto's illegitimate son, could be anything more than a New Order stooge.

While doubts concerning the legitimacy of Habibie's birth were wholly unfounded, his presidential legitimacy was a subject of serious debate at the highest levels. The student activists, among others, believed Habibie's inauguration ceremony in the presidential palace, seconds after Soeharto's resignation speech, was not valid, as it was not conducted in the MPR assembly hall as stated in the constitution. This was a bit disingenuous of the students, as they were occupying the MPR complex at the time.

The various student protest committees planned a city-wide series of marches, sit-ins, and rallies aimed at speeding the transition to full democracy. This time around, the students had no intention of remaining on campus. Favored venues were the boulevard facing the presidential palace, the expressway in front of the MPR, and, guaranteed to cause the most disruption of urban life, the Hotel Indonesia traffic roundabout, a bottleneck for almost all downtown traffic.

Heri soon found himself in the center of the action. Trisakti alumni supporting the student movement knew Heri was young, smart, energetic—and presently unemployed. They asked Heri to assist in logistics support for the rallies. It was no easy matter getting thousands of students into the streets and keeping them fed, watered, and, as much as possible, under control.

Heri plunged into his new volunteer role, spending most of his afternoons and evenings in the student command centers or in a specially marked van parked on the demonstration route. I applauded his enthusiasm, even when he phoned at three a.m. asking for help rounding up five hundred packages of rice and eggs for breakfast. Hearing the breathless, commanding urgency in his voice, I marveled how an apolitical, materialistic Indoyup could be transformed into a social revolutionary in less than a year.

The second round of student demos were colorful affairs. Participants from the major universities wore jackets identifying their alma maters, creating seas of canary yellow and sky blue. Those from the specialized institutions brought their distinctive characteristics: waist-length hair and headbands of the art college students, secretarial school students in high-heels and tailored office wear, future hotel industry professionals in chef's hats and waiter's vests.

If enthusiasm was high among the participants, as well as among television news crews assured of getting good footage with minimal effort each day, other Jakartans were less than amused. Street-side polls revealed that most people thought hampering business by disrupting traffic was not the way to get the nation back on its feet. As usual, taxi drivers were the first to grumble. Living on the knife edge, handling hundreds of thousands of rupiah a day only to be left with a pittance after paying the rental fee and fuel, the drivers complained bitterly of long waits in congested traffic and declining numbers of passengers.

Most surprising was the opposition from the street scavengers, the *orang kecil*, the little people presumed to benefit most from a truly representative, socially responsible government. Several score of scavengers staged a counter-demonstration at municipal hall, disparaging the students as spoiled, middle-class brats with no feeling for the daily struggle endured by most Jakartans.

The students were not the only groups disrupting city life. The South Jakarta municipal government was compelled to address the contentious issues stemming from the kafé tenda popping up every night on Kebayoran's once-tranquil avenues like mushrooms after a spring rain. Some streets became impassable from sunset until well after midnight, forcing residents to park a hundred meters or more from their homes. In the early evening, crowd noises and cooking smells permeated the air, lending the genteel neighborhood of stately mansions and rambling bungalows the atmosphere of an amusement park. Toward midnight, students, artists, and other denizens of the night replaced the early-evening clientele of families and young professionals, forcing the good citizens of Kebayoran to rub shoulders with the bohemian classes when returning home after hours.

The city fathers were in a bind. Work days became a succession of vaguely intimidating telephone calls from affected residents, which included many senior military officers. After the discovery of used syringes and condoms on the grounds of an adjacent mosque, local religious leaders marched on city hall demanding that Kafé Tirtayasa be closed, and, according to one report, that the slutty starlets running the establishments be flogged for good measure.

The Kafé Tirtayasa operators, especially those who were respectable businesswomen like Yani, were understandably offended. Yani joined many of her follow operators in a counter-protest march on City Hall. Dressed for action in designer jeans and T-shirts, they sang rousing tunes proclaiming the basic human right to make a living, not to mention, according to one observer, the equally unalienable right to keep up payments on the BMW.

Caught between annoyed residents, self-righteous religious leaders, and prickly celebrities, the city fathers scrambled for a compromise solution. They finally decided to convert several unoccupied public areas for use by kafé tenda, by arranging utilities, sanitary facilities, and adequate parking. Yani elected to move her café to the spacious park surrounding Monas, the last of former President Soekarno's bombastic monuments to nationalist glory.

When I was downtown, I would often grab an early dinner at Yani's instead of fighting fifteen kilometers of traffic to the Kemang Palace. There is a touch of magic about Monas at sunset. The marble monument and surrounding broad avenues and spacious lawns are bathed in a golden glow reflected from the plate-glass façades of the office towers ringing the square. Hurricane lamps from dozens of mobile food stalls form a necklace of brilliant white stars along the promenades.

Like a village square, Monas attracts street people, laborers, and low-income families from many areas of Jakarta. They squat on the sidewalks or sit on straw mats laid on the grass, enjoying a weekly outing or, for some, an infrequent and much-anticipated treat. But walking south a hundred meters brings you into a far different world, the Kafé Monas, where chairs and tables replace straw mats and wooden benches. Instead of the soothing hiss of hurricane lamps filling the night air, cell phones beep for attention with the urgency of life-sign monitors in a cardiac ward.

The two worlds did not coexist peacefully. Kafé Monas was in operation only a few days when the roving food vendors who had worked around Monas for years complained that the new establishments were taking away customers, neglecting to consider that few of their regular patrons could afford the kafé tenda overpriced offerings.

It was a turf war. Despite sporadic official attempts to clear the ambulatory food sellers, beggars, and prostitutes from this symbolic center of the Indonesian nation, Jakarta's underclass had claimed Monas for themselves. They were not pleased to see suburban Indoyups encroaching on their territory.

Monas was not Jakarta's only venue for class struggle that month. Tensions rose in the Kemang Palace immediately after Adam's arrival. I ran the Kemang Palace on the understanding that if a steaming cup of coffee was waiting on the terrace table when I staggered downstairs in the morning, I would take a lenient attitude toward any lapses or omissions made by the staff during the rest of the day. Occasionally, waking before my accustomed hour, I would hear Pak Tatang hounding Inem to ensure the coffee was ready. Then they knew they could relax.

Seeing how efficiently the staff organized my morning coffee, Adam assumed they would be equally conscientious throughout the day. Taken individually, none of his demands were excessive. But putting them all together was too much for the staff to handle. The problems started the morning of his residence, when Adam, clad only in sarong, appeared at the door to his room and berated Inem for not having installed toilet paper in his dispenser.

I was to blame for the oversight. All the bathrooms in the house contained what Siti and I considered perfectly adequate, Asian-style personal hygiene facilities. Inem, who had never worked for a westerner, was confused and distressed at Adam's anger. Siti took Inem aside and calmed her down while explaining the problem. Inem went to the store later that day, returning with several rolls.

She obviously wanted to make a good impression on Adam, to make up for what she still believed to be her own mistake. That night, she cooked her favorite chicken recipe, so juicy and sauce-laden that finger bowls are always supplied. To ensure Adam was fully satisfied, Inem went one step further, placing a fresh toilet roll at Adam's place on the table, so, Inem thought, he could wipe his fingers in his accustomed manner.

To be fair, Adam did try to mold Inem into his version of a perfect *pembantu*. One afternoon, I left my office and stuck my head over the mezzanine railing to ask Inem to make me some ice tea. Inem was standing in the living room, with some amusement watching Adam iron a business shirt while giving a running commentary on the proper technique. Engrossed in his task, when Adam heard my voice he did not realize I was, in fact, calling to Inem. When he put down the iron and looked at me expectantly, I said, "Not you, the other pembantu."

Money, that scarce commodity during Krismon, was also an issue. As an academic on sabbatical, Adam considered himself on a restricted budget, though his savings, sabbatical honorarium, and small research grant, when converted into rupiah, added up to a generous monthly allowance by my penurious standards. Since Adam considered Siti a permanent resident, he would only agree to pay a third of the utility bill. By the same token he proposed to pay only a third of the staff salaries, less an additional sixteen percent to account for the five days Pak Tatang spent in his home village each month. This would have been acceptable, except as a condition of his residence Adam insisted I service his bedroom air conditioner and water heater, neither having been used in over two years. I believed this to be a trivial expense, as home service charges, being mostly labor, had not risen greatly during Krismon. However, I forgot that the freon used in air conditioners is imported. The electric water heater proved to need a complete overhaul when a trial run provided a spectacular fireworks demonstration caused by combining cheap plumbing and faulty wiring with several years of neglect. After totaling the service bills and calculating the utility payments based on the increased usage, I discovered Adam would have to reside in the Kemang Palace for at least two years before I realized any profit.

While I resigned myself to the situation, not willing to threaten a long-time friendship over such a vulgar matter as money, Siti proved much less accommodating. She recoiled in genuine horror as a full gamelan was moved into the house. Though Siti's family is from Yogyakarta, a major center of Javanese culture, she cannot abide anything Javanese, even complaining, only partially in jest, to the word "java" on my favorite Starbuck's coffee mug. For Siti, music was MTV and the traditional culture of Java was as foreign to her as the polka would be to an alternative rock fan.

The open-air design of the house—the sign of true tropical living—effectively eliminates privacy. Sound from one corner of the house carries through all living areas. When he was at home, Adam spent much of the day listening to tapes of gamelan and other traditional music, which impinged on Siti's enjoyment of MTV, causing her to jack up the volume. Adam would compensate by increasing the volume on his stereo.

My motivation for moving into the Kemang Palace was not—or at least was only partially—to enjoy expatriate comforts I could not otherwise afford. I needed a place to work that was both quiet and provided ready access to commercial districts, so I did not waste potentially productive hours travelling to and from client meetings. The Kemang Palace, initially a haven of tranquility, could now be as noisy and distracting as my downtown rented room. I would often step through the front door, craving peace and quiet after an exhausting day of meetings and travel, only to be assaulted by the computer-made clamor of modern pop counterpointing the gentle but forceful rhythms of the gamelan.

Ita

THE ENGLISH AND THE JAVANESE, two insular peoples living at opposite ends of the Eurasian landmass, have a lot in common, at least in their upper social echelons. The England and Javanese aristocracy have both raised hypocrisy to an art form, believe they are the most civilized people on the planet, and repress emotions to the point of neurosis. As a result of their perceived superiority, both England and Java have absorbed their immediate neighbors into unified political entities ostensibly to the benefit of all, though the affected populations have somewhat different opinions about the arrangement.

During September and October 1998 there arose another striking similarity between the two societies. The best English comedy counterpoints sidesplitting farce with brutal violence. In this regard the situation in Jakarta during the second half of 1998 can be best described as Pythonesque.

During our frequent afternoon coffee breaks at Trisakti, Monica and I amused ourselves by reading newspaper articles aloud to each other. Monica, who does a hilarious imitation of a pompous government official, had great fun parodying official pronouncements regarding a perennial issue, the ban on *becak*, Jakarta's version of the pedicab. For two decades the Jakarta municipal government has been attempting to remove becak from city streets, where they provide convenient, affordable transportation, especially in back alleys too narrow for other public vehicles. The official reason for ridding the city of becak was that the sight of a sweating *tukang becak* propelling a corpulent passenger supposedly epitomized, in some official's memorable phrase, "the exploitation of man by man." I suspect city officials wanted the becak gone because they were a constant reminder that "the exploitation of man by man" is also a fitting description of the New Order's style of government.

One afternoon, Monica read to me a newspaper advertisement for stainless-steel chastity belts. The belts, leather-lined and equipped with state-of-the-art electronic locking devices, had a slim profile, guaranteed invisible under office and casual wear. I was about to make a tasteless joke about the wearer forgetting the pass code during the passion of her wedding night when Monica's smile suddenly vanished. Her voice and expression grew solemn as she read aloud a report of a teenager found stabbed in her bedroom when her family returned home after an afternoon shopping trip. Police believe the girl, Ita Martadinata, had surprised a burglar ransacking the supposedly empty house.

Both of us suspected there was more to the story. The article mentioned Ita had been a rape counselor, but Monica and I wondered how many teenagers would be up to the demands of counseling women who had suffered violent sexual abuse, especially considering the sheltered upbringing of most middle-class

Indonesian girls. Monica studied the photo accompanying the article. To her, Ita's Chinese features suggested the possibility she actually had been a rape victim, as the great majority of reported cases involved ethnic Chinese victims.

Our idle speculations deepened into suspicion the following day when an unemployed neighbor confessed to the crime. A facetious rule-of-thumb states the faster the arrest and easier the confession in a police case with no eyewitnesses, the more likely the alleged perpetrator is a convenient scapegoat. The newspaper report also mentioned Ita had been scheduled to fly to the United States with her mother to give testimony on the rapes to a human rights investigation group.

Subsequent reports detailed a rather lurid sexual history for a Catholic schoolgirl. Since most Indonesians tend to hold conservative views about sexual behavior, suggesting a young, unmarried woman such as Ita had had any sexual experience at all was a serious accusation. To accuse her of practicing sodomy, as did the police the day following her death, was out-and-out character assassination.

Then the story vanished from the local media, despite sufficient potential to keep the tabloids supplied with the prurient, sensationalist articles that is their mainstay. This sudden silence was reminiscent of similar cases during the New Order years, when a killing perpetrated by the drug-addled child or jealous wife of a high official would be resolved with an innocent bystander incarcerated and a few vaguely threatening calls to editors burying the story.

I noticed a change in Monica during subsequent days. Brooding silence had replaced lively banter as she withdrew into herself, venturing only monosyllabic comments bordering on rudeness. I wondered if, like me, she was disturbed that the unanswered questions of Ita's death, the rapes, and other atrocities were no longer even being asked.

Farid was also troubled by Ita's death and the general disregard of the rape issue, but was more philosophical. Farid thought the rapes would quickly vanish from the public consciousness because the issue is commonly regarded as a "Chinese" problem, tangential to the real concerns of the Indonesian nation.

Farid told me how the various appalling incidents in Indonesian history tend to become trivialized. As an example, he mentioned acquaintances, all highly educated, who honestly believed that only a few thousand people had been killed during the anti-Communist pogrom in the mid-sixties. In fact, the lowest independent estimates put the number of deaths in the half-million range.

With few exceptions, the foreign press did not seem interested in pursuing the stories. The international celebrity correspondents had moved on to other trouble spots, and the resident correspondents were concentrating on reporting and analyzing efforts to rebuild the economy and develop workable civil institutions. Still believing I am actually a journalist despite all evidence to the contrary, Farid suggested that I investigate the Ita story myself, both to satisfy my own curiosity and as a sort of tribute to one more victim of Indonesia's continuing social upheaval.

I saw Monica smile for the first time in a week when I told her of my intention to conduct my own freelance investigation into Ita's death. Her first words were: "You will need a photographer."

We began our search for the truth by visiting Ita's neighborhood, an area called Tebet, where I also had once lived. Established in 1962 to house lower-class residents evicted to make room for a hundred-thousand seat stadium—another of Soekarno's grandiose monuments—Tebet has become one of Jakarta's many upwardly mobile neighborhoods. Though houses still stand cheek-by-jowl along narrow alleys, creating an urban kampung, many Tebet families have found success in the vibrant economy, and the strategic location has attracted affluent young professionals.

Most Tebet homes have acquired a second story or have been completely rebuilt. The alleys off the main roads, designed for the becak, now banned, are slalom courses of parked vehicles. Homeowners who have transformed their front patios into minuscule carports must thread their family-sized vans through the alley, half of the tire tread hanging over the drain, to squeeze through the gate with scarcely a centimeter of clearance.

With no response to repeated knocks on the Martadinata front door, we sought background information from neighbors. All we spoke with agreed the Martadinatas were, in every respect, a normal family, which is probably why they were so astonished when the police called on every house in the street to carefully explain how this earnest Catholic schoolgirl had practised sodomy.

Though the slanderous stories of Ita's supposed sex life were certainly fabrications, an additional piece of information we acquired that day was not so easy to dismiss. A neighbor told us that Ita's mother belonged to one of the several groups assisting rape victims. In the days after the first reports of mass rape, over-eager activists had done their cause a grave disservice by releasing unconfirmed figures and dubious, sensational accounts—such as stories of family members forced to perform sexual acts on one another at gunpoint—from purported eyewitnesses.

The discrediting of these initial reports a few weeks later only supported the government's views that the rapes either did not occur or were, at most, sporadic, isolated events. Though official denials and rumor-mongering by the military were all common practices during New Order times, I realized there remained the real possibility that Ita's death was unrelated to the rapes, and the family was leaping to conclusions, as other activists had done earlier in the year.

Monica and I decided to determine how many atrocities alleged to have occurred during the riots could be confirmed by impartial means. Through his student contacts Heri put me in touch with Anwar, a human-rights activist who claimed to have verified a number of rape cases. I made arrangements for Monica and me to visit his home in a crowded East Jakarta neighborhood. We were ushered into his office, then ushered out again when we realized it would be too much trouble to shift the piles of documents lying everywhere to make a place for us to sit.

After making us comfortable in the common room, Anwar showed us a printout of fifty-eight eyewitness accounts, all obtained either from the victim herself or from a bystander. I read a couple of pages. Though all accounts seemed plausible, none had corroborating evidence. Anwar then brought out photographs taken during the riots. Most of the photographs of looting and vandalism were authentic—I could recognize specific buildings I had seen myself on that day. A few depicted unconscious women lying on the roadway or sidewalk, one with her shirt hiked up to the waist to show blood-stained underwear. Looking at a particularly gruesome photograph of a naked corpse on a morgue table, I remembered I had seen that same image on a website documenting alleged atrocities in East Timor. If including this unrelated shot in the collection was only an honest mistake, it still underscored the necessity of rigorous confirmation of all evidence.

Monica asked if she could meet any rape victims herself. Anwar explained how he and his colleagues refused access to victims to spare them needless trauma. Monica said she understood, but her face showed her disappointment. I suppose Anwar was impressed by this young Chinese Indonesian searching for truth for its own sake, because he phoned Monica two days later, offering to arrange victim interviews under conditions of strict anonymity.

No men were present as these interviews, only Monica and a rape counselor. Those interviews were almost as unbearable for Monica to hear as the women to recount. Through habit, she had brought her camera, though doubting any of the subjects would agree to be photographed. To Monica's surprise, several did consent, almost eager to show the world their violation.

One of the victims stripped naked for Monica's camera to show scars on breasts, vagina, and buttocks, as though the violence had rendered her sexually neutral, exempt from an Asian woman's normal modesty. Monica left the interview with renewed determination to discover the truth.

Soeharto's Fishpond

WHILE MANY YOUNG COUPLES continued a fruitless quest for employment, Heri and Yani were as busy as during their Indoyup days. Besides the kafé tenda, Heri devoted most of his time to student protest support activities. Yani had found a new source of income, selling discount cosmetics directly to formerly big-spending friends unable to do more than window shop at their favorite department stores.

Then, in late October, disaster struck as Heri and Yani lost their two live-in pembantu. The teenage girls, who were cousins, had been ordered by their family to return home to Cirebon, a harbor town three hours east of Jakarta. This traditional center for rattan handicrafts had become a Krismon boom town as the overseas demand for rattan furniture soared. As most stages of rattan furniture manufacture are carried out in home workshops, the family needed every available hand to help with this tedious, exacting work.

The shrinking of Jakarta's normally huge floating population of rural migrants was creating a serious pembantu shortage, one of the many paradoxes of Krismon. Though beggars and hawkers filled the streets, servants with good references were hard to find. Yani arranged for a neighbor's pembantu to do essential housework like cleaning and laundry, but shopping and care of Satria fell to Yani, and, on days when she was on sales calls, to Heri.

Heri was a natural at child care. Though not exceptionally gentle or sensitive, he became an excellent parent to Satria, at least in Indonesian eyes, by treating his son like a little prince, slavishly indulging every whim.

Shopping was another story. In the local supermarket, Heri would stand, transfixed, staring at long shelves filled with bottles and boxes of products with catchy names and obscure functions. At any rate, to save money Yani told Heri to by-pass the supermarket in favor of the traditional wet market for most of their fresh food requirements. On the days Heri held shopping duty, he was so overwhelmed by the market—the noise, smells, and mud—he would grab items from the stalls nearest the entrance and thrust the asking price into the vendor's hands before beating a hasty retreat. The vendor, annoyed Heri made no attempt to bargain, as good manners dictate, would mutter complaints about the Indoyups being little better than foreigners.

Generally, Satria would spend the day with his grandmother, so Yani could make sales calls and Heri concentrate on student support activities. The various organizations were planning a series of mass rallies to commemorate the anniversary of Sumpah Pemuda, the date in 1928 when youth groups swore an oath to uphold "One Nation, One People, One Language." By the time of the Sumpah Pemuda rallies, the object of student protests had shifted from a generalized dissatisfaction with the present government to focus on a security bill being deliberated in the legislative assembly. The government argued the new bill would replace the draconian regulations in effect since the Soekarno years, insisting all nations, even model democracies, have some sort of security regulations on the law books. The students were having none of it. Having grown up with official perfidy, the students could not take any government announcement at face value.

On several occasions during those weeks, Heri and I would meet at the café, him returning from a day in student organization headquarters or on the streets while I was finishing equally grueling meetings with my clients. Heri was concerned about the increasing incidents of food poisoning from meal packages donated to student organizations. All incidents were minor, many probably attributable to the casual Indonesian attitude toward hygiene.

Heri once said, only partially in jest, that the students were poisoning each other. Though everyone described—or complained about—the student demonstrators as though they were a single entity, the movement was as fractious as Indonesian society itself. From fundamentalist Christian and Islam groups to neo-socialists, the students pursued widely differing agendas, united only in their hatred of the status quo.

Heri related humorous stories of constant bickering among the various groups. I was reminded of the Chicago Seven Trial in 1968, in which a group of student activists were accused of conspiring to disrupt the Democratic Party convention being held in that city. The most vocal of the accused, Abby Hoffman, dismissed the charges by stating conspiracy implies a group of people agreeing on a certain course of action. Well, Abby said, the Chicago Seven could hardly organize a conspiracy to overthrow the government when they could not even agree on where to have lunch.

Fractious as it was, the student movement in Jakarta was also notable for a high degree of unity, tolerance, and common purpose. Young people from throughout the archipelago worked shoulder-to-shoulder; priests were invited to address Muslim student groups. Inter-ethnic and religious rivalries faded into insignificance as the students fought to keep the nation they would one day inherit on the road to reform.

Aware that the students were putting the New Order's slogans promoting national unity and inter-ethnic tolerance into enthusiastic practice, I was shocked when a student organizer chatting with Heri and I at Yani's café suddenly complained about "niggers." I gently corrected him, assuming he meant "Nigerians," but he insisted on using a word that would bring him serious risk of injury if overheard in western cities.

In fact, he was referring to some West African customers at a neighboring café. Africans were an exotic new addition to the Jakarta scene. In the months after the rupiah's plunge, textile traders from many West African nations had set up export businesses in Jakarta. Indonesian batik is fashionable in those countries, and the rock-bottom prices created fine opportunities for small-scale trading.

After a few months, the lucrative trade attracted others besides legitimate businesspeople. Accounts of the susceptibility of many Indonesians to con games aroused the attention of swindlers, drug dealers, and other criminals. The legitimate traders clustered in hotels around the textile markets in Tanah Abang. The less salubrious gravitated to Jalan Jaksa, where hotels and restaurants served budget tourists and a raucous nightlife provided ample opportunity for criminal behavior.

The atmosphere at Jalan Jaksa subtly shifted from laid-back neo-hippy to American inner city. Fights, refusals to pay for meals, and other incidents strained the Javanese attitude for black-skinned people, which at the best of times would put a western racist to shame. Jalan Jaksa's most popular café posted a sign stating, in English, "We don't serve Black People. Too much trouble."

Adam told me he saw this sign one evening while seeking an inexpensive late dinner after attending an official function at a nearby government office. Adam was dressed, appropriately for the occasion, in a batik dress shirt. Taking advantage of the situation, he also wore a *peci*, Indonesia's national headgear, to hide his bald spot. Save his white skin and prominent western nose he was the very image of an Indonesian government official.

Speaking flawless, unaccented Indonesian, Adam berated the mystified manager for violating the nation's SARA laws, which proscribe serious penalties for disparaging written or oral comments based on race, tribe, religion, or ethnic group. Adam returned to Jalan Jaksa a few days later, and noticed that the sign had been removed.

Had the SARA laws been impartially enforced in the Kemang Palace, Pak Tatang, Inem, and even Siti would have been incarcerated weeks ago for disparaging remarks against Caucasians—one in particular. Exasperated with his nitpicking habits, the servants had squared off against Adam, with Siti as an avid ally. Adam would emerge from his morning shower to find nothing but damp towels, Inem having neglected to hang them in the sun the previous day. His room was left uncleaned for days, shirts were ironed sloppily or not at all, his evening meal was swimming in grease. When Adam complained, with justification considering he was contributing to her salary, I asked Inem for an explanation. Her only reply was *"rasain,"* serves him bloody well right.

Generating this much enmity was a major achievement. For all the dire warnings in guide books and cross-culture behavior manuals about the dangers of being an overbearing foreigner, it takes quite an effort to annoy most Indonesian employees seriously. In fact, the running battle between Adam and Inem was a new twist on the traditional relationship between servant and master. As is fairly common among foreigners pursuing a serious interest in Javanese culture, Adam had adopted many of a Javanese gentleman's distinguishing traits. Adam was not being pretentious, or at least was being sincere in his affectation. He honestly believed that the arduous process of ingraining gentle behavior and excruciating politeness into his brash American manner was demonstrating his deep respect for the people whose culture had so enriched his life.

A noble sentiment, but unfortunately Adam had somehow also adopted the upper-class Javanese disdain for household staff. While Adam and Inem grumbled in private about each other's shortcomings, his relationship with Pak Tatang was openly hostile. Convinced the old man was chiseling him while running errands, on his return Adam would carefully count the change, scolding Pak Tatang as though he were a child if he so much as deducted money for ojek fare.

The worst instance was the drama resulting from Adam's request for Pak Tatang's assistance in building an authentic screen for a *wayang kulit* performance. One of a gamelan's primary functions is to provide the musical accompaniment for the wayang, the mythic puppet theater at the heart of Javanese culture. To raise the prestige of his own gamelan orchestra, Adam pursuaded one of Indonesia's top *dalang* to employ his gamelan group for a televised wayang performance.

. Like professional jazz musicians who know a repertoire of thousands of songs by heart, good gamelan players can participate in a wayang performance without ever having previously worked with or even met the dalang. Nevertheless, Adam insisted on recreating a typical wayang venue in the Kemang Palace living room for a full rehearsal.

Adam ordered Pak Tatang to construct a *layar*, a screen made from white canvas stretched on a bamboo frame, with a banana tree log at the base to hold the puppets when not in use. However, budgeting any type of construction during Krismon was impossible. Though the government tried to control the market of basic goods, the prices of anything not considered essential to daily life fluctuated wildly, sometimes on a day-to-day basis. Bamboo stems, banana tree logs, and screen fabric were definitely in the non-essential category. Adam gave Pak Tatang a budget, which the old man discovered was completely inadequate on his first trip to the construction materials shop. When Adam accused him of inflating the prices in collusion with the shop owner, Pak Tatang complained bitterly to me, his honor impugned by the accusation of petty thievery.

The situation was exacerbated at the end of October by the disaster every Kemang household dreads: the departure of domestic staff. Inem had been requested to return to her home village for some unclear reason during the period Pak Tatang would be away on his regular monthly trip to his own village. Entreaties to both to delay one or the other's departure fell on deaf ears. Pak Tatang's village was awaiting his money, seemingly on the brink of starvation, while Inem's summons was equally urgent. I let them go, figuring we were not so spoiled we could not handle doing our own housework for a week.

With Siti and me home all day, finding time for household chores was not a problem. We shared general cleaning duties, with her handling the laundry, as she did not trust me with her knock-off designer wardrobe. We assumed Adam would clean his own room and otherwise take care of himself.

As both Siti and I love to cook, we decided to collaborate in the kitchen. We had few opportunities to indulge our hobby when Inem is in residence as the pembantu strongly objected to incursions into her territory. I would feel uncomfortable even making a sandwich with Inem glaring from her perch on the back stairs. Siti and I planned a week of culinary adventure, with Adam as a beneficiary, since preparing a third portion of a meal involved trivial extra effort.

During that week, Adam would return home to a meal of grilled free-range chicken with Javanese vegetable salad, or a three-course Mediterranean dinner. I gave Siti a generous shopping budget, which resulted in her returning from one trip to the supermarket with a box of imported pancake mix. A few weeks before I had related fond childhood memories of my uncle cooking huge farm-style breakfasts on Sundays and holidays. Siti brandished the pancake mix, insisting I teach her how to make a Canadian Sunday breakfast.

I could not refuse. Though I have survived quite happily on Indonesian food for two decades, I still cannot face a plate of rice for breakfast. I make do with boiled eggs and bread. If I could teach Siti the secrets of a western breakfast, she could pass the recipes on to Inem, enabling me to indulge myself every Sunday with a soul-warming feast.

Siti got the hang of this unfamiliar cuisine immediately. The bacon—actually smoked beef strips in deference to Siti's religion—was crisp, hash browns not greasy, pancakes light and spongy, toast slightly browned, and fried eggs glistening. It was perfect in every detail. Only after a week of such breakfasts and gaining three kilograms did I make Siti understand that the key characteristic of the Canadian Sunday breakfast is, unless you are a farmhand, that it is only served on Sunday.

Such breakfasts are made to linger over, so each morning Adam and I put off work so we could indulge ourselves in a second cup of coffee and a chat. Since Adam's fluency in the Javanese language, mastery of Javanese etiquette, and deep familiarity with traditional culture gains him entry into the highest social circles, I could enjoy inside stories of the elite jockeying for position in the post-Soeharto power structure or trying—with little success—to determine the direction their nation was heading.

One morning, after finishing a hilarious story about Habibie once being mistaken for his own son, Adam casually mentioned he was down to his last clean shirt and his room needed a good sweeping. He looked significantly at Siti, who in turn looked in me, but said nothing. I let the matter drop, but when Siti complained the next day about the difficulty she was having ironing Adam's shirts properly, I hit the roof. I reminded her that she was a resident of the Kemang Palace, not a servant. Adam had no right to assume she should fill in for Inem just because she is a young, female Indonesian. I muttered something about neo-colonial attitudes and returned to work.

My casual dismissal of the problem plunged Siti into a serious dilemma. Taught from birth to serve her elders and trained in the hotel industry, she felt duty-bound to do as he asked. I felt she should confront Adam, just say "do it yourself." But she could not bring herself to stand up to a man her father's age. Instead, she avoided direct confrontation by doing as Adam wished, but broke off all further communication with him.

The "cold war" between Adam and Siti put me in the unenviable position of peacemaker. I did not consider asking him to find alternate accommodation. For me, at least, he was good company. I enjoyed our reminiscences of Indonesia in the eighties, and we discussed the current situation far into the night. In addition, a steady stream of visitors from all traditional artistic disciplines greatly enhanced the atmosphere of the Kemang Palace.

I appealed to Siti to exercise more patience. After all, I reasoned, since academics are often forgetful, and artists self-absorbed, Adam, being both, might be expected to be a less-than-ideal housemate. But Siti, as an *anak bungsu*, the youngest child in an Indonesian family, believed she had a culturally sanctioned monopoly on self-centered behavior. I could only hope that when Inem and Pak Tatang returned from their respective home villages their presence might help restore harmony in the Kemang Palace.

When they did reappear, coincidentally both on the same day, they came with extra baggage. Inem brought along with Darto, whom she claimed was her husband, and Pak Tatang arrived with his nephew Uus, who wanted to search for work in Jakarta. The two new occupants only increased the tension in the Kemang Palace. Pak Tatang suspected that Inem and Darto were not married, though Inem insisted they had married at their district Islamic affairs office. Siti suggested Darto was a relative masquerading as a husband so he could enjoy free room and board while looking for work in the capital.

Pak Tatang continued to show his displeasure during subsequent days, complaining that Darto did not show him the proper respect. Inem of course, took Darto's side, and the atmosphere grew frosty in the staff quarters.

The atmosphere was not much better in the master bedroom. My ongoing investigation of the truth behind the May Riots resulted in lengthy telephone conversations with Monica. Siti was not amused to hear me in animated conversation with an attractive young woman about wholly unfamiliar subjects. Whenever the telephone rang, Siti would leap to answer. If the caller was Monica, she would have to undergo an extended interrogation before Siti let me take the call. Siti made frequent references to my "girlfriend" and, in true Javanese fashion, retreated into sullen denial whenever I claimed we were only professional colleagues.

To escape the tension I would retreat to the back terrace, where Siti's chance discovery of a goldfish bowl hidden in a kitchen cabinet had led to a hobby which had grown completely out of hand. The single bowl, long since broken, had become two aquariums and a fish pond, a small marine park to which many visitors to the Kemang Palace liked to contribute new inhabitants. I suppose they thought a goldfish was an acceptable dinner-party gift now that wine was prohibitively expensive.

The diverse population created a logistical nightmare, as every species seemed incapable of peaceful coexistence with the others. Siti's favorites, the Koki with their ornate fins and coloring created by intensive inbreeding, needed climate-controlled conditions to survive, requiring a tank for themselves. In the other tank, angel fish would eat the fry of the goldfish; the iridescent *golsom*, a gift from Siti's father and therefore not to be considered a candidate for the frying pan, savaged everyone.

I tried subdividing the pond with wire mesh to create my own fishy subdivisions where all could live in splendid isolation, but every few days a turtle, a house gift which had taken to hiding in the drain pipes, would stage a midnight raid, taking no prisoners. As I tried multiple configurations without success, I gained renewed respect for old Bapak Soeharto and his three decades as paterfamilias over two hundred million squabbling children.

Indonesian Dating

A FEW YEARS AGO, shortly after I had my divorced my first wife, I made my first hesitant re-entry into the Jakarta singles scene. I chose one of my favorite places of ten years previously, Tanamur, the legendary discotheque whose clientele encompassed all levels of Jakarta society, from street hookers to the children of the elite. Though the dance floor is the most spectacularly democratic in the city, different groups tend to coalesce around specific areas, reducing the risk of misunderstanding—not to mention assault or deportation—if, for example, a clueless foreigner tries to pick up a general's daughter.

I was having a drink at the back downstairs bar—a designated free pick-up zone—when I started chatting with a young woman on the next barstool. My experiences of meeting women in bars before my marriage led me to expect little more than an exchange of personal information. Within minutes, I was astonished to find myself discussing chaos theory as a tool to determine the probable paths of several foreigners cruising the bar for someone to cuddle with in their over-air-conditioned hotel rooms. My new friend proved to be fourth-year mathematics student out on the town with a classmate to celebrate the high grades they had achieved on their mid-term examinations.

This was the first indication that I had entered a whole new world. When I first arrived in Jakarta, most foreigners' relationships with Indonesian women took place in shabby, dimly lit bars, which suited the oil workers, who constituted most of Jakarta's single foreign male population at the time, just fine. By the early nineties, when the thriving non-oil sector attracted a wider variety of single expatriate males, many young mainstream Indonesian women, especially those educated abroad, formed serious relationships with resident foreigners. However, sex was seldom part of the arrangement—at least in the beginning.

Some of these girlfriends tried to find a workable compromise between eastern values and western expectations. One popular solution was simply putting a halt to sexual activity at an arbitrary point during foreplay, leading to men in their thirties to relive painful teenage memories of acute frustration in the back seat of the family car.

One of my first Indonesian girlfriends had a more culturally appropriate solution. She offered to select a bar girl for me to satisfy my carnal desires, a novel variant on the traditional practice of a Javanese wife, who, after reaching a certain age, will find a suitable second wife for her beloved husband. Though I appreciated the gesture, I declined, thinking it too bizarre even by my jaded standards.

These days, cosmopolitan young women like Siti tend to regard virginity not as a prize to be zealously guarded until marriage as much as a condition to be discretely remedied at the appropriate time. Though serious relationships with foreigners which are based on mutual respect and affection are increasingly the norm among educated Jakartans, some bars are still filled with bule-hunting sirens accompanying Western men well past their prime of physical appeal.

Siti is scathing in her contempt for these bar bitches, as she calls them, probably because, at first glance, she could easily be mistaken for one. Siti favors short, tight skirts or hip-hugging jeans and a skimpy top showing off a bare midriff. When going out, she usually insisted I wear a sports coat, not for my own benefit, but so she can borrow it to cover up if we found ourselves in a place where such attire would have been inappropriate. Only her well-modulated speech and demure mannerisms indicate she does not spend half her life shouting to be heard above the raucous din of a disco sound system. Whenever I was annoyed at Siti or in a sadistically playful mood I would loudly mispronounce a few common Indonesian words in a public place, as though I were a tourist she had met in a bar the previous evening.

Most of our friends and acquaintances regarded Siti's presence in the Kemang Palace as no more remarkable than a western woman openly living with her partner. Family and neighbors were another matter. Fortunately, many young urban women have developed several effective techniques to maintain discretion. For example, many boarding houses catering to students or career women have at least one "ghost" occupying a room paid for each month but seldom used.

Since initially she slept at the Kemang Palace only a few nights each week, Siti would tell her family she was staying the night with a fellow worker whose house was located near the hotel. This is a common ruse. One young woman carrying on a lengthy affair with an expat convinced her family she was sleeping over at various friend's houses for over two hundred consecutive nights.

A few weeks after we met, Siti's hotel closed one of its two Executive Lounges, since very few businessmen were willing to conduct business in the strife-torn archipelago. The hotel could offer Siti nothing more than a waitress position, for which she was overqualified, so she accepted a severance package and resigned.

With no reason to leave the Kemang Palace in the morning, all pretense was dropped. Siti moved in most of her wardrobe and other belongings, converted the guest room into a dressing room, and adopted the role of Lady of the Manor so expertly I decided not to correct tradesmen and neighbors who addressed her as my wife.

A week after Siti had taken up permanent residence, her eldest sister visited the Kemang Palace. Insisting we sit in the stuffy front reception room instead of the cool back terrace, to underscore the formality of the occasion, she asked my exact intentions concerning her baby sister. Considering the state of the economy and my own precarious finances, I felt I could hardly make a commitment beyond promising to "do the right thing," not mentioning that I had no idea exactly what the right thing might be.

Siti was helpful, suggesting a type of Islamic marriage called *bawah tangan*, which simply involved giving some money to a religious official. I demurred, as the term means something like "underhanded" or "under the table" and the perfunctory ceremony is disconcertingly similar to a midnight wedding in Las Vegas without an Elvis impersonator conducting the ritual.

In the absence of plans for the future, Siti and I took the path of least resistance, known in Indonesian as *kumpul kebo*, living like buffalo, which signifies living as man and wife without benefit of clergy. In doing so, we made our contribution to the rampant misunderstanding and confusion regarding relationships between Indonesian women and foreign men, which many believe to be based solely on money.

The prevalent mercenary view of mixed couples explains why Siti would never admit she was relieved when my financial position improved. Unlike the early days of Krismon, corporate copywriting now provided far more than a survival income. Student protests notwithstanding, the stability and promise of free elections spurred a dramatic resurrection of the rupiah during October. Everyone seemed to have shaken off the doldrums, and was trying to get the economy running again.

For me, corporate copywriting used to be a necessary evil, a way of keeping rice on the table between more interesting writing assignments. During this stage of Krismon, however, copywriting had become a suitable outlet for my creative urges. Indonesia's battered business community needed a deft and imaginative touch to reassure customers and stockholders of their continuing viability in the midst of crisis.

I relished the challenge of finding the exact turn of phrase to explain how their company's technical bankruptcy—the situation resulting when the rupiah value of foreign-denominated loans far exceeded the company's entire book value—was actually nothing more serious than a temporary liquidity problem. Conversely, companies with predominantly export markets needed to convey the impression that triple-digit increases in profit were a product of visionary, astute management, not the dumb luck of skyrocketing net returns caused by the plummeting rupiah multiplying the value of foreign revenue while slashing rupiah-based operating expenses.

With some money to spare, I was no longer a *bule kere*; I had become Bank Bule. Though no one I knew would believe my financial condition was only marginally better than dozens of Indonesian banks being closed down, forced to merge, or taken over by the government, I was regarded as the lender of first—and last—resort.

I came to dread an unexpected knock at the door of the Kemang Palace. Since the neighboring houses were empty, and friends would phone before dropping in, a knock on the door was either Adam having forgotten his keys or someone asking for money.

Beggars or con men were not a problem. Pak Tatang would chase away anyone without written authorization from municipal authorities to canvas households. Authorized supplicants were generally neighborhood organizations soliciting money for social activities. I was glad to help out for children's games days and the like, though it could get expensive. Since the amount of each contribution was public knowledge, I had to at least match the offer of my most generous neighbor.

Otherwise the supplicants would be from Siti's family. Besides medical treatment, I was called upon to finance birthdays, circumcisions, and more obscure ceremonies. I also was required to attend those functions, it not being sufficient that I helped sponsor them. I could hardly refuse, as being a ready source of money seemed to be the only basis on which Siti remained on good terms with her family while openly living with me.

I thought the issue was over until one night a couple of weeks after she moved in. By coincidence, the plots of two different television programs Siti and I watched were mawkishly sentimental stories about newborn babies abandoned through improbable plot twists. I suppose this triggered a maternal response in Siti, for later that night she asked if we could have a baby.

I froze, my perennial inability to sort through the Indonesian language's ambiguous verb system leading me to believe she was already pregnant, despite our precautions. My relief at learning the truth gave way to renewed concern when I discovered that Siti was dead serious about wanting to become pregnant with little delay. I tried to convince Siti of the utter impracticability of starting a family now, even ignoring the fact we were not even married. While my income had improved, inflation was keeping us only a half-step ahead of bankruptcy. Besides Siti, Inem, and Pak Tatang, I seemed to be supporting most members of a West Java village, considering Pak Tatang's constant requests for advances on his salary. We had nothing left over for unforeseen expenses, such as medical care, which was soaring. Though I could depend on affluent friends for an emergency loan in case of accident or illness, I doubt anyone would shell out for Siti's visits to an obstetrician.

"No problem," she told me, "the neighborhood midwife can deliver the baby." A recent magazine article about rising newborn mortality rates during Krismon flashed through my head as I imagined Siti lying on a bamboo pallet in a dirt-floored hut screaming while a cackling village crone brought our child into the world. I was going to argue, then thought better of it and kept my silence, aware through experience that my western concepts of common sense were of little use in this strange territory.

In some Jakarta neighborhoods, turning a corner on a busy street will bring you into a quasi-rural setting where farmers tend crops in tiny lots nestled behind modern commercial buildings. Occasionally, conversations with educated, westernized Indonesians offer a similar phenomenon, as in a science-fiction story where an inter-dimensional gateway on a non-descript city street thrusts an unwary pedestrian into a parallel universe. It is as though you were walking along a bustling street filled with late-model automobiles, modern electronic goods in shop windows, bookstores and newsstands offering contemporary informed knowledge and opinion—and then, with no warning, the conversation takes an abrupt turn and you are in a kampung, chickens and naked tots running at your feet, smoke from wood fires swirling around your head, the surrounding forest filled with malicious spirits.

Siti's and my hypothetical offspring-to-be dominated our conversation for days. Siti insisted her biological clock was ticking fast; I countered by saying that at twenty-four, her clock was only just being wound up. In fairness, Siti was only a victim of rural Javanese values, which demand a woman begin her reproductive life in her late teens to ensure enough hands to help in the rice fields by the time the parents reach their thirties. Well-researched and forcefully presented arguments outlining how advances in health care and greater longevity have extended prime childbearing years into the early thirties for most women had no effect on Siti's conviction that she was on the verge of a barren spinsterhood.

She insisted that all Javanese women believe their quarter-century mark to be the onset of old age. I tried to test Siti's hypothesis during dinner at a Kemang café, when we were invited to join the twenty-fifth birthday celebration of the owner's daughter. I knew the young woman to be Javanese, so I asked her, with Siti within earshot, if a twenty-five-year old person was young or old. She looked slightly confused, then replied: "Young, of course." I turned to Siti with a smile of having made a point. She replied, in a dismissive tone, "She obviously didn't understand the question."

At a loss, I did something I have not done since I was a teenager: I turned to my mother for help. For some weeks, Siti, Mom, and I had been carrying on a lively Internet chat exchange, late morning coffee here being Mom's Happy Hour in Vancouver. During one session, I suggested that Siti ask my mother for advice, considering she would become a grandmother. To Mom's credit, she scarcely paused when, in the middle of light chatter, Siti typed "Would you mind if I had Jeremy's baby?" After confirming she read the message correctly, Mom promised to reply by e-mail the following day.

The e-mail message carefully and sympathetically explained to Siti that taking on such a responsibility in a time of economic crisis was folly. I printed the message out, so Siti could read it in private. Shortly after she settled on the back terrace to read the message I heard a gasp of surprise, then silence. A few minutes later I looked out of the office window to see Siti burning the message in the barbeque pit.

For days after that incident I was reluctant to return home and face Siti's sullen resentment, born of a belief that my mother and I were conspiring to frustrate her natural reproductive drive. When not passing time at Yani's café, I would sit in bars, nursing a beer and looking wistfully at the middle-aged expats and teenage bar girls at adjacent tables. To amuse myself, I tried to determine which of these mutually exploitative relationships might mature and grow into mutually exploitative marriages. I imagine a significant number of such unions are successful. For the girl, the regular remittances to her family secure peace of mind and respect in her community. In return, the man acquires a sort of bargain-basement trophy wife, the kind of gorgeous young woman a middle-aged man at home can acquire only after amassing millions, available here to anyone with the proven ability to hold down a decent job.

What is Truth?

GROWING DEMAND FOR MY COPYWRITING SERVICES—I was one of the few professional English-language writers still in Jakarta—forced me to spend as much time out of the house attending meetings as at my desk doing productive work. However, the chaotic traffic conditions resulting from the continuing round of demonstrations defeated all attempts to organize my day. I would often arrive at a client's office after the meeting had ended, or show up on time to be told the meeting was cancelled because other participants were trapped immobile on some distant roadway.

After years of resistance, I finally surrendered to the necessity of buying a cell phone, which allowed me to minimize wasted time and rearrange my schedule on the fly by keeping in constant touch with clients and colleagues. Siti, of course, wanted her own cell phone, arguing that no woman should travel through Jakarta's now-dangerous streets without being able to call for help. I could not argue, but told her she would have to pay the usage bills herself, an agreement that was quickly forgotten.

One day, I phoned Siti's cell phone when she was an hour late for a dinner date. Hearing the irritation in my voice, Siti assured me she was sitting in a taxi five minutes away from the restaurant. On impulse, I then phoned the house number. Siti answered. As usual when I caught her in a blatant lie, she giggled and changed the subject.

I could only sigh and move on. Falsehood, equivocation, and vagueness are fundamental to Indonesian—particularly Javanese—social intercourse. The Javanese believe telling someone an unpleasant or disturbing truth violates every tenet of civilized behavior. Javanese mendacity exasperates many Westerners—and Indonesians from cultures where direct expression is the norm—who regard habitual lying as a moral deficiency.

On the other hand, these believers in the sanctity of truth might themselves lie to their adopted child about his true parentage, or conspire with a doctor to give a false, reassuring prognosis to a terminally ill patient. The Javanese only take this concept to the logical extreme, placing a person's short-term emotional tranquility above all other considerations. As a former girlfriend once told me, "*bohong itu benar*," lying is right.

I still cannot accustom myself to being lied to for my own good. To achieve some sort of balance, I became obsessed with finding the truth behind the May Riots. I spent most of my free time combing through back issues of newspapers and magazines, trying to extract information of value from a welter of contradictory reports, statements, and analyses. According to the government, the May Riots were the result of economic desperation which ignited long-standing tensions between Chinese and pribumi Indonesians. The opposing view stated that the kidnappings, lootings, and atrocities were a full-scale military operation directed from the highest levels.

Witnesses described many of the rioters as well-built, short-haired, and acting in a disciplined, organized manner—in other words, like trained soldiers. They claimed these men had directed rioters to loot and burn specific shops and stores. Rape victims and eyewitnesses insisted that in most cases, the assailants were not common rioters.

At first, the government issued a categorical denial of any systematic sexual assault during the riots. Later, as more eyewitness reports surfaced, government spokesmen admitted some rapes might have occurred, with the possible involvement of soldiers acting outside of the chain of command.

Many commentators opted for an explanation acceptable to all parties—the government, military, and rights activists—that the May Riots and other nefarious military excesses were the work of Prabowo Subianto, a powerful army general married to Titiek, Soeharto's second daughter.

I paid special attention to these charges because I was acquainted with several people who knew him, including former subordinates. I could not believe the intelligent and cosmopolitan career officer they remembered, who placed the comfort and safety of his troops over his own, could be the same near-psychopath capable of organizing and executing the rape and slaughter of hundreds.

On the other hand, acquaintances and former subordinates alike related stories of Prabowo's fearsome temper. I also know he holds some rather extreme views regarding the supposed Chinese' domination of the Indonesian economy. Even so, Prabowo's exile to staff college and subsequent formal expulsion from the military without any form of trial or investigation too much resembled a setup. I wondered if Prabowo, the "soldier's general," might have suffered the same fate as Ita Martadinata's supposed murderer, or if he was the quintessential symbol of his people, a face of sophisticated culture and great civility concealing a heart of brutal savagery.

As I was returning home from a client meeting one afternoon, my taxi was halted as waves of demonstrators passed along the sidewalk and between the lines of cars. Needing some excitement after many frustrating days spent in fruitless library research, I thrust a five thousand rupiah note at the driver, jumped from the cab, and followed the crowd.

I felt comfortable and secure in this carnival atmosphere. Students and other demonstrators waved at me as I passed, ojek drivers clustered in groups, handy substitutes for the taxis and buses trapped in the traffic gridlock on adjacent streets.

Closer to the police lines the mood shifted as demonstrators threw rocks and police responded with tear gas. The crowd behind me was growing dense as demonstrators pressed forward. I doubted I would be able to fight my way against the flow, so I followed other journalists behind police lines for protection. I noticed all the journalists, domestic and foreign, were wearing laminated press tags around their necks. A sergeant approached and asked me who I was. When I replied that I was a journalist, he demanded to see my press tag. When I said I had left it at home, he told me to get lost.

"We can't protect you if we don't know who you are."

The sergeant hailed one of the many ojek clustered behind police lines and ordered the driver to take me to a safe location. Grumbling, I mounted the motorcycle and we sped off. A few hundred meters from the demonstration, the streets showed no sign of the thousands of massed students and security forces just around the corner. I tapped the driver's shoulder and motioned for him to let me off at the taxi stand just ahead, where several drivers were leaning on their vehicles, chatting amiably.

When I pulled out my wallet, the driver told me I owed him twenty thousand rupiah, about four times the usual fare for that short distance.

"*Harga demo*," he explained, which probably meant "special price for spiriting idiot foreigners away from riot zones."

When I told Farid about the incident the following day, he mildly berated me for running around without accreditation, saying it marked me as an amateur. If I was to be a serious journalist, I needed some sort of official recognition. He suggested I visit Pak Adé, an officer at the Department of Information he had once met through a journalist friend. Even though I was not attached to any official news agency, Pak Adé might be able to arrange some sort of special accreditation.

The next morning, for the first time since my days as a travel journalist, I stepped through the door of the dreaded Department of Information. I remembered being treated with suspicion on my previous visits, having to grovel at the feet of officious functionaries and endure detailed scrutiny of my professional background, such as it was. Foreign journalists told me those days were over. They described the warm smiles they received while being issued press credentials, which they got as easily as movie tickets.

Deppen, as the Department of Information is

commonly known, was undergoing profound changes under the ostensibly reform-oriented government. Yunus Yosfiah, the new minister, had become the bright, shining star in Habibie's administration. Though Deppen could claim a distinguished origin as the sole voice informing the world that Indonesia had a legitimate and effective government during the revolution, under the New Order it had been degraded to a propaganda tool, whose primary role was to stamp out any and all expressions of free speech.

The Indonesian word for information, "*penerangan,*" is based on the Sanskrit root "*terang,*" meaning "light." In the Indonesian language, the addition of prefixes and suffixes can add auxiliary, sometimes abstract, meaning. In this case, a literary interpretation of *penerangan,* with its mystic overtones of spiritual enlightenment, yields the ironically appropriate term "absolute truth."

For three decades, the "Department of Absolute Truth" had vigorously stifled free flow of information in all directions, hammering newspapers into submission with threatening telephone calls to chief editors, and obstructing or even banning foreign journalists. Through direct control of all television and radio news broadcasts, most Indonesians heard a version of current events having only a passing acquaintance with reality.

The stringent policies designed to stifle press freedom had also become a lucrative source of income. Deppen functionaries profited from growing public literacy by charging exorbitant fees for the few publication licenses available. Foreign news and documentary crews were compelled to take along, and pay for, a minder who would ensure that no images deemed disparaging to the Indonesian nation would be captured on film or video. One of my duties as occasional local liaison for film crews was to momentarily distract the minder when they wanted to grab a forbidden shot.

Since the fall of Soeharto, Deppen became a vanguard of reform within the system. Yunus, an active army officer who, ironically, was suspected of responsibility for the 1975 deaths of five Australian journalists in East Timor, systematically rolled back most restrictions on the content and licensing of print media. After decades of maintaining a firm stranglehold on the Indonesian press, Deppen was fading into irrelevance.

Though I knew Deppen had changed, I also remembered that department functionaries had particular contempt for freelancers, reflecting the Indonesian distrust of an individual not subordinate to a formal organization. So, with some trepidation, I entered the portals and groped my way through labyrinthine, dimly lit corridors, searching for the elusive Pak Adé. Kafka came to mind as I asked in several offices where I could find him. All knew of him, but none seemed to know where his new office was located.

I stumbled on him almost by accident, as I peeked behind a wall of shelves dripping with tattered files. Dressed in a crisply laundered safari suit, Pak Adé was balding, with the sallow look of a lifetime paper pusher. For better or worse, this was where my search for press accreditation would end.

It is considered bad form to immediately state your business to a government official or other highly placed personage unless you know him well. First, you make small talk, and wait for the official's invitation to state your business. Depending on his rank in relation to your own, his current mood, the time of day, and the importance of other items on his schedule, this preliminary period might last anywhere from ten seconds to an hour.

Pak Adé obviously was in a mood to talk, and had time of his hands. Instead of showing the slightest curiosity about my visit, Pak Adé launched into an extended narrative about Deppen's chaotic reorganization. In a voice reflecting astonishment and disbelief, Pak Adé related how the previous week, rank-and-file bureaucrats had voted to disband the Deppen chapter of Korpri, the compulsory association of civil servants.

After almost twenty minutes, I risked committing a grave faux pas by broaching the subject of my visit myself. When, in a roundabout manner of course, I inquired about the possibility of obtaining some sort of official recognition, Pak Adé's face assumed a stern expression as he straightened and sat back in his chair. He slowly and systematically enumerated the grave consequences I would face if I tried to act as a journalist without the proper accreditation.

"The regulations are very strict on these matters. If my colleagues at Immigration discover you are working without proper accreditation, you will be deported."

Seeing my downcast look, Pak Adé's face softened.

"Don't worry," he said. "We need people like you to tell our side of the story. Besides, *anda tahu sopan*, you have good manners. So many of these foreigners march in here and demand accreditation, like we are their servants."

As we were discussing possible options I could explore to provide the necessary foundation for granting me a press pass, a travel agent courier arrived with an envelope for Pak Adé. Excusing himself for the interruption, he opened the envelope and examined the contents: three airplane tickets. As the courier left, he wished Pak Adé a pleasant stay in Bali.

I inquired if he often went to Bali. Pak Adé looked embarrassed, saying he owned a house there, where his wife wanted her and the children to stay during the MPR session, as she was afraid of possible street violence. The meeting ended, Pak Adé told me to return after the MPR session and he would see what he could do.

Kafé Monas is a short walk from Deppen, so I went to Yani's café for a late-afternoon coffee. Heri was also there, having just finished fieldwork for that afternoon's demonstration. He laughed when I related the visit with Pak Adé, saying: "He is just fishing for money. What *pegawai negeri* can afford a house in Bali?"

The threat of deportation was enough to curtail my journalistic impulses—until Anwar telephoned a few days afterward with news of a rioter, recruited from outside of Jakarta, who might be willing to tell his story. The meeting, arranged through one of the more radical activist organizations, took me to a world I had often spied from a distance, but had never visited—squatter settlements on the banks of the Ciliwung, the river flowing through the heart of the city. The taxi driver was not familiar with the area, so I alighted in the general vicinity and searched for the address on foot. As I crossed a bridge to the opposite side of the river, I could see clapboard huts clinging to the muddy river banks, supported by stilts seemingly in danger of dissolving in the black water oozing toward the sea. The mud-filled alleys reeked of cheap cooking oil and inadequate sanitation.

Unlike the bright concrete walls of houses in other kampung, these dwellings showed little evidence of maintenance or more than superficial cleaning. Interiors were almost unlit, containing at most plastic chairs or a threadbare mattress. This was the world of Jakarta's floating population of millions of rural residents who come to the city for a few months to work at menial jobs, returning to their villages to let others take their place scraping a meager existence.

There were few of the exuberant greetings from the residents I had come to expect when I walked through more affluent urban kampung. Asking around, and hearing answers laced with suspicion, I found the address, where Anwar waited with my interview subject. I sat on the floor, and tea in a stained cup was placed in front of me. Reflecting on the probability the water to wash the cup and perhaps even to make the tea came from the river, I was for once relieved that proper etiquette demanded I wait for the invitation to sip my drink, and wondered if somehow I could avoid touching the dodgy brew altogether.

The young man had the short stature and tight build of someone accustomed to hard labor with minimal nutrition. He seemed fearful; Anwar had to assure him repeatedly that I could be trusted. He explained that he had been recruited by an army sergeant at his village in the neighboring island of Sumatra to burn down a major department store. When the store was in flames, he and his fellow arsonists tried to run outside, but were stopped by the soldiers, who forced them back inside at gunpoint. He was the only arsonist with the courage to jump through the flames to the back of the store, where he smashed open a small window and leapt to safety, suffering a sprained ankle as well as second degree burns and smoke inhalation. The others cowered in the burning structure until the roof collapsed. Since then he had hidden in Jakarta, certain the soldiers would kill him if he returned to his home village.

I pressed him for further information: which store? the name of the sergeant? was he from Kopassus, the army's elite commando unit, or a regular soldier? He refused to answer. When I turned to Anwar and said I had heard enough, the man shouted "I'm not lying!" and removed his shirt to display burns on his left arm and left side of his torso. To my inexpert eye, the scar tissue looked fairly recent, plausibly dating from the previous May. I also noticed several transverse scars across his inner forearm, too shallow and in the wrong position to indicate a failed suicide attempt. Marks like those are usually caused by cutting shallow incisions with a razor blade to rub low-grade heroin under the skin.

I looked into his eyes. If he did use heroin, was he a hard-core junkie with a good story to sell to a gullible foreigner, or a terrified young man far from home?

I repeated the fugitive arsonist's story to Pak Trisno later that afternoon, and asked the old journalist if he thought the account was true.

"Sounds likely," Pak Trisno said. "The army has a long tradition of using street thugs for their dirty work."

I sat upright. "Then I have a hot story! It proves the army was behind the riots."

Pak Trisno smiled. "It proves nothing. Even if your friend is telling the truth, maybe someone hired the sergeant to burn down his competitor's business."

"But that's a good story, too!"

"Certainly, and you might make headlines. But the government and military would just deny all your allegations. In a week, everyone would forget."

I slumped in my chair. "I guess you're right. And Immigration would deport me for practicing journalism without the proper visa."

"How would that make your nice young lady feel? You have a good life here, my friend, and we need you."

"I know. I have to support Siti and most of her clan."

Pak Trisno chuckled. "I meant in a larger sense. Look around."

He motioned toward the open doorway to his shop. I saw the fine furniture sets on display or piled to the ceiling, awaiting shipment.

"All these items are hand made, by common Indonesians in villages and towns throughout Java. I help provide a livelihood for maybe a thousand people."

"That's good," I agreed, "especially now, during the crisis."

"I am successful in my business not because I am an honest man, though it helps, certainly," Pak Trisno said, with a slight smile. "I am successful because God has seen fit to bless me with the ability to converse with my customers intelligently, often in their own language. This gives them confidence that I know how to run my business and maintain international quality standards in the goods I manufacture."

I nodded, while wondering, as I often did when conversing with Pak Trisno, where this was leading.

"A small businessman who speaks only Indonesian or simple English will find it hard to attract potential customers amid global competition. However, future customers often learn of a company through reading a leaflet or advertisement. By hiring you to write these materials using proper spelling and grammar, a factory owner indicates he pays attention to detail, which helps create a good first impression."

I was flattered—sort of. I had often been complimented on my style and imagery. This was the first time since the fifth grade I had been praised for my spelling.

"Every business you help to sell goods in overseas markets creates jobs for many people. The smaller the business, the more money goes directly to the people who need it most. That is your real contribution to my country, not exposing the truth or teaching us the errors of our ways."

"You don't think it is important to search for truth? After all, sir, you were once a great journalist."

Pak Trisno nodded slightly at the compliment.

"Not a great journalist, just a good one, at least according to my readers. A good journalist is very clever at finding the truth. A great journalist knows that the truth is only what people chose to believe."

Monica was not happy about my reluctant decision not to publish the results of our investigations.

"We must do something," Monica pleaded. "Everyone will just forget."

I did not repeat Pak Trisno's observation that people would forget anyway. Not wanting to meet her gaze, I studied a montage of photographs of the university campus and newspaper clippings on the opposite wall, a student project from several years before. I smiled at the decade-old headlines, reliving my own memories of the period. That gave me an idea.

I suggested that Monica create her own photomontage by juxtaposing her self-documentation images with other print materials. As I gave her a few ideas, I saw Monica's eyes light up for the first time in weeks.

Monica decided to produce her montage on computer video, asking my assistance to alter and animate the images. I enjoyed not having to be creative for once, concentrating only on developing the techniques for translating her vision into a dynamic montage. I discovered that a sophisticated sense for moving composition complemented Monica's talented eye for framing still images.

Our first effort portrayed the environment where the rapes had occurred, but it did little to illustrate the soul-wrenching depravity of the act itself, which Monica needed to convey if her work was to have lasting impact. Swearing me to secrecy, Monica showed me her photographs of rape victims. We agreed they should be included, but only, of course, if we could conceal the women's identities.

I helped Monica digitally dismember the rape victims, allowing her to use the haunted eyes, the mouths pursed in pain, the burns and jagged scars on limbs and torsos. The more shocking images appeared for only an instant, already gone by the time the viewers realized they had seen mutilated genitalia.

The resulting video was better than either Monica or I had expected. By using dismembered body parts as fleeting images, barely glimpsed, Monica had expressed the ultimate degradation of rape: the reduction of women to disjointed components, to be used and discarded with casual cruelty.

Mean Streets

LIKE MOST JAKARTANS, I have difficulty hanging on to material goods. Money disappears from wallets, gold pens leap from office desks, compact disk collections shrink in the humid climate. Indonesians generally attribute these miraculous phenomena to mischievous *tuyul*, light-fingered elves. Supernatural or not, the petty thief often plaguing my daily life must be brighter than one passerby, who entered my house in Tebet some years ago through a door carelessly left open. Seconds later, the pembantu entered the front room and screamed when she saw the intruder. Panicking, he grabbed the first item within reach, which happened to be a television remote control, and fled. Unfortunately, that remote control device was for use with a European-manufactured television I had bought from an expat selling his household goods before moving to another country. No other remote could be programmed to work with this particular television, and I assumed the stolen device could not operate a locally manufactured unit.

At any rate, that inconvenience was trivial compared to what I suffered one morning shortly after moving to Jakarta. After spending several futile minutes groping around the shelves of the shared bathroom of the *indekos* where I was staying, I realized someone had stolen my contact lenses.

Until Krismon, crime victims in Jakarta generally must endure little more than this sort of senseless exasperation. Since aggressive or violent robbery was not common, I, for one, did not hesitate to stroll through the streets at any hour. Of course, I took care not to set myself up as a target. I dressed casually, put my watch in my pocket, and carried myself as though I were perfectly familiar with the area, even when hopelessly lost in a maze of alleys.

As poverty and desperation worsened with the deteriorating economy, I found myself constantly looking over my shoulder. Each day's newspaper carried reports of robbery with violence: watches snatched from pedestrians on main roads at midday, ojek riders knocked on the head and pushed off their machines, bus passengers threatened by parang-wielding gangs.

Victims were not the only ones at risk. Newspapers also carried gruesome reports of criminals caught in the act being literally torn apart or burned alive by enraged local residents. One thief got off lightly when his intended victim tossed chilli powder into his eyes. The bystanders, who would normally have pummeled the criminal, only watched him scream and writhe in agony, perhaps thinking this was punishment enough.

As newspaper headlines screamed "City of Fear," middle-class Jakartans looked askance at every seedy or unfamiliar character. I was no exception, having a seedy but all-too-familiar character residing in the Kemang Palace staff quarters. Darto was making no progress in his search for employment, presumably through lack of effort. He lazed around the staff quarters, or would disappear entirely for a couple of days. Pak Tatang shared my distaste for Inem's putative husband. Whereas Darto was superficially respectful to me, he was openly dismissive of the old man. I would often hear Pak Tatang grumbling to himself about Darto's attitude.

Darto's lack of manners did not concern me as much as the possibility he might soon investigate less legitimate types of employment. Farid glibly suggested he could earn extra money stealing automobile side mirrors. The soaring cost of luxury auto parts had opened up whole new career opportunities for petty thieves. In pre-Krismon Jakarta, only a parked, unguarded vehicle was at risk of losing a tape deck, or, in some models, the entire dashboard. Now, some congested intersections had become notorious for the street thieves who would surround cars stopped in traffic and, as the occupants cowered inside, unfasten the side mirrors and sprint away. More aggressive robbers would smash car windows with a rock or hammer and snatch cell phones from terrified passengers. I cautioned Farid not to give Darto any ideas.

I was more concerned that Darto might try his hand at home burglary, another Krismon growth industry. Burglaries are usually inside jobs, in which a pembantu leaves the otherwise unoccupied house unlocked, then takes a convenient afternoon nap. Though Inem came with impeccable credentials, I worried Darto might send her on an errand while his new friends waited outside.

At least Uus, Pak Tatang's nephew, was a welcome addition to the growing Kemang Palace family. This naïve and good-hearted eighteen-year-old would leap to attention, ready to be of service, whenever I so much as glanced in his direction. Pak Tatang tried to find Uus a position watching over one of Kemang's many unoccupied houses, and implored me to cast around my expat friends for office-boy work. When not job hunting, Uus helped Pak Tatang and Inem with household duties. He faithfully followed his uncle to the mosque, and I would often find them both praying in the garage, or discussing Islam in the context of daily life.

For Darto, Uus, and other uneducated, inexperienced country boys, the employment situation was not entirely bleak. When either Darto or Uus disappeared for the entire day, I assumed they had joined the thousands of jobless Jakartans paid a few thousand rupiah to parade around downtown streets promoting one or another group's interests or agendas, a sort of rental demonstrator.

The round of demonstrations and counter-protests was gathering steam in anticipation of the MPR special session scheduled for mid-November. As the highest political body in Indonesia, the MPR meets every five years to elect the president and vice president, and to determine the overall guidelines for governmental policy during the subsequent presidential term of office. Besides these regular events, the MPR may also meet at any time in special session to address situations affecting the entire nation.

The upcoming special session was intended to enact the requisite legislation and set the timetable for a general election that all hoped would be more democratic than the government-orchestrated affairs held during the Soeharto years. Proposed changes in the electoral law included allowing the establishment of other political parties besides the three existing parties sanctioned by the New Order government, setting up an independent electoral commission to conduct the elections, and to permit local monitors and foreign observers to oversee the entire process.

The students were not impressed by these ambitious plans for instituting full-scale democracy, believing the Soeharto-picked MPR members would only attempt to turn back the clock. Demands by students and other community groups to include more radical reformist measures on the agenda were ignored, sparking a new, more strident round of demonstrations. In return, security authorities threatened harsh measures against those intent on "disturbing the public order." The stage was being set for another showdown between the students and the army.

There was also widespread concern about social unrest during the session. Recently there had been several incidents resembling gang fights between residents of adjacent neighborhoods in the city's poorer sections. Many observers believed provocateurs were fanning long-standing feuds to create havoc, maybe intending to create a favorable environment for Soeharto's return to power.

Farid was watching the news when I dropped in one afternoon. Looking at the television image of rough-looking, raggedly dressed men being herded onto the back of a truck, I remarked on the military's good sense to round up potential troublemakers ahead of the MPR session.

"Those aren't troublemakers," Farid said. "They are helping the military keep order."

Farid explained that the army had decided to augment the thinly dispersed regular troops by recruiting hundreds of rural unemployed people into a paramilitary force eventually called Kamra. As Kamra recruits were not allowed to carry guns or knives, many armed themselves with *bambu runcing*, a long bamboo stake with one end carved into a sharp point. As I watched the television, I remembered Pak Trisno telling me about the army's penchant for using civilian thugs. Images of last May flashed through my head as I wondered if the students may not be right after all.

Street thugs were also worrying Yani, who had lost most of her enthusiasm for her café. The downtown location attracted large crowds, but few customers. Where Kafé Tirtayasa in suburban Kebayoran Baru offered a convenient neighborhood rendezvous, getting to Kafé Monas involved a major excursion from most residential areas. Kafé Monas visitors seemed less interested in socializing over coffee than strolling around hoping to glimpse a favorite singer or television star waiting tables or cooking fried rice.

The location itself posed another problem. The area is notorious as a venue for beggars, prostitutes, and other less-wholesome Jakartans. Kafé Monas organizers decided to fight fire with fire, in this case a candle with a flame thrower, by hiring unemployed youths hanging around the nearby Tanah Abang market as their security force. These louts, called *preman* from the Dutch word for "free man," lounged near the parking lot or strode among the cafés, emanating a palpable sense of menace.

Two months into operations, Yani had heard these *preman* grumbling about late salary payments. This was idiocy of a high order, to hire a street gang for security and then neglect to pay them. Yani decided to close her café and concentrate on direct sales of cosmetics,

helping friends and acquaintances organize afternoon
house parties where she might sell up to a million
rupiah worth of cosmetics and toiletries.

Encouraged by her success, she branched out into
a similar activity: commission selling of life insurance
policies. Interest in life insurance was growing among
the middle-class as the economic crisis underscored the
need for long-term financial planning. Selling life
insurance involved working most evenings, explaining
the intricacies of term policies to both husband and
wife. As the MPR special session neared, Heri was also
out every day, often staying away far into the night
preparing for the following day's demonstration.

This brought Heri and Yani into conflict. Since
the Indonesian Bank Restructuring Agency had tracked
down and repossessed the luxury sedan Heri enjoyed
as an executive perk, their sole transportation was a
Kijang van, Yani's mother's wedding present and
formerly Yani's personal vehicle.

While Heri generally let Yani take the Kijang for
after-dark sales calls, one evening Heri insisted he
needed the car to transport leaflets and other materials.
Before Yani could argue Heri had taken the keys and
walked out the door. Grumbling, Yani phoned a taxi
to take her to a customer's house in an outlying real
estate development. When they arrived, she asked the
driver to wait for her. He refused, explaining he had
been driving for twenty-four straight hours and was
due for his shift change.

When Yani finished with her client she phoned for
a taxi, but none of the companies could send a vehicle
to this outlying suburb in less than an hour. Anxious
to return home, Yani decided to walk the few score
meters to the main road and stop a cruising taxi. Yani

peered down the dark street with a strong sense of unease. She knew she was taking a risk, as hailing a taxi in Krismon Jakarta is not to be undertaken lightly.

Taxis are a perennial source of exasperation for Jakarta residents, Indonesian and expat alike. Before Krismon, the passenger might suffer, at most, a surcharge from the driver taking an unnecessarily long route to the destination. Often this was unintentional, as the expanding taxi fleets were forced to hire drivers with minimal knowledge of the sprawling capital's convoluted road system. Since the start of Krismon, however, taxis had been implicated in a spate of nasty incidents, including the death of a Japanese resident expat and the kidnapping of a German tourist. Honest drivers, working eighteen-hour days to bring home a pittance over the daily rental fee, were in equal jeopardy. Newspapers frequently carried reports of a luckless driver found knifed to death in his taxi, killed for literally a few dollars.

Yani had already experienced one minor incident. She had placed her groceries in a cab, then realized she had left one small bag on the check-out counter. She asked the driver to wait, but when she returned, the taxi—and her groceries—had disappeared.

With both driver and passenger potential victims, flagging a cab in some neighborhoods became a kind of mating ritual, like two people meeting in a bar trying to determine whether the other is genuinely looking for a fulfilling relationship or is a serial killer. To avoid attracting the driver's attention as the taxi approached, would-be passengers peered into the middle distance, as though waiting for a friend, while furtively trying to determine if vehicle and driver were in reasonably good condition. At night, all pretense was discarded as both parties warily regard each other while weighing respective alternatives of a long walk home and forgoing a badly needed fare over the real possibility of armed robbery.

The only taxi to appear after a fifteen-minute wait was from an unfamiliar fleet, one of many licensed to operate in the outer suburbs. As the vehicle seemed in good repair and Yani did not relish another long wait on this empty suburban roadway, she motioned the taxi to stop.

Yani was relieved when the driver claimed familiarity with her neighborhood. Nevertheless, she paid close attention to the driver, making sure he took the most direct route. A few minutes into the journey, Yani noticed the driver was in the wrong lane for the turn they should take. She politely reminded him, but the driver refused to cut across traffic, and they missed the turn.

Yani berated the driver in a sharp voice, telling him another turn lay ahead. However, he maintained a straight course, sailing through that intersection without reducing speed. When Yani insisted the driver turn around, the driver launched into a petulant monologue condemning her and all of her class.

"You rich bitches think you know everything," he said, "and we are nothing but dumb coolies. Well, I may just be a little guy, but I have my self respect. Don't try anything with me."

Yani gripped her knees and forced herself to take several deep breaths as the driver ranted. When her panic subsided, she considered her options. Leaping from the vehicle was out of the question. The driver had turned onto a multi-lane main road with no traffic lights and was maintaining a good speed. Half-expecting an accomplice hidden in the trunk to push his way into the passenger compartment, Yani reached into her samples bag, finding a can of anti-perspirant. If the driver slowed the taxi at some point, she would spray it into his eyes, hoping he would hit the brakes in panic and stop before he ran off the road or into another vehicle. It was risky, but she was terrified that he might enter a dark side street or take her out of the city, where an attempt to escape on foot would be futile.

The driver suddenly ceased his tirade. Yani looked through the front windshield to see the flashing lights of a police roadblock. Yani relaxed her grip on the spray can and sat back in relief as her taxi was pulled over.

With a week to go before the MPR session, the police had set up check points to keep track of potential troublemakers suspected to be flooding in from other areas of the archipelago. Never willing to pass up an income-generating opportunity, they were also collecting money from taxi and public-transport drivers.

Without a word, Yani dropped a few small rupiah notes on the front seat, opened the door, and stepped out. She thought of telling an officer about the incident, but realized she could not prove the driver was guilty of anything other than bad manners and a lousy sense of direction. Instead, Yani walked a few steps to where a brand-new taxi from a reputable company had also been pulled over. Seeing the cab was empty, she stepped in and gave the uniformed driver a twenty thousand rupiah bill—the smallest banknote remaining in her wallet—indicating he should give the money to the police officer at his window. The driver and police officer, both familiar with the protocols of roadside extortion, protested the bill was too large, but Yani was insistent. The officer shrugged and accepted the money, then the driver took Yani home.

The next morning, Yani's mother visited to hear the story of the previous night's adventure. Afterward, when Yani was out of the room, she insisted to Heri that he give Yani priority in the use of the car. Heri countered that theirs was a modern marriage, in which he and Yani had equal rights over all property.

"You start bringing in half the family income," Yani's mother said, "then you can start talking about equal rights."

Heri had no answer, and could only nod in mute agreement. For several days afterward he brooded about his loss of status in his own family. Krismon had claimed another victim.

Black Friday

A KNOCK ON HIS BEDROOM DOOR two hours before dawn
aroused Monica's brother from sleep. Monica was
standing at his door, holding a can of shaving cream
and a razor, asking him to shave her head bald.

Monica did not provide any coherent explanation
for wanting to lose the jet-black, silken hair she had
treasured since childhood. Her brother woke their
parents and convened a rather groggy family meeting,
eventually reaching a compromise, as was their custom.
Monica's mother fetched a comb and scissors; ten
minutes later all but one centimeter of her daughter's
long, glossy hair was on the floor.

Monica's economics-faculty classmates offered
guarded compliments on her punk crew cut. The fellow
members of her photography club, on the other hand,
were openly delighted. Monica had become something
of a star in the graphics faculty; her video essay had
impressed and moved many Trisakti students and
instructors.

Monica wore her transient fame lightly. After
completing the video, she felt little inclined to
continue her self-documentation project. She was also
dropping behind on her schoolwork, unable to focus
on learning arcane economic theories after her soul-
searing experiences with rape victims.

A chance encounter with a student-activist organizing committee member led to Monica's involvement with the student movement. Conscious of their role as standard bearers for reform, Trisakti students were converting their campus into a support base for the MPR demonstrations, the third major focus of student activity along with the University of Indonesia downtown campus and Atma Jaya University on Jalan Sudirman. Besides enjoying prestige as top-rank universities and having strategic locations in central Jakarta, these campuses share another important attribute. All three institutions are adjacent to large, well-equipped hospitals.

As with her radical new hairstyle, Monica offered no clear explanation for her involvement in the student protest movement. Her friends attributed the decision to stress, the Indoyups' catch-all explanation. For whatever reason, Monica launched herself into support activities with the same enthusiasm she had shown during our abortive investigation of the May Riots.

For most of November, Monica's family saw her only when she stopped by the house for a quick wash and a change of clothes. On some days she would bring a shopping list for food her fellow activists needed at the command center or on the front lines. Though her brother complained about the imposition, their mother would fix dozens of box lunches without protest, often spicing up the menu with her home-made Chinese sweet cakes.

As expected, the level of violence in the student demonstrations increased as the MPR session approached. The first sign of trouble came when a student driving an open-roof Volkswagen Safari ran into a group of soldiers, injuring several of them, as he made a panic-driven flight from other security personnel who had been pounding on his car—and him.

Every afternoon traffic on Jalan Sudirman and adjacent roads would grind to a halt as demonstrators thronged the avenue. When the MPR session opened on 10 November, the military sealed major intersections and instituted a containment policy based on strategic retreat. On each day of the session, the demonstrators would be halted at a pre-determined point. Then the troops would fall back to another point a few hundred meters closer to the MPR, giving the students a sense of progress and accomplishment. On each successive day, the troops would hold their final line closer to the MPR complex. If all went well, on the final day of the session the students would reach the MPR main entrance, just as buses full of delegates were driving out the back gate.

Unfortunately, Indonesian military strategy suffers the fate of most of the nation's efforts at sophisticated logistics and organization. The plan looks great on paper, but something always breaks down in practice. As the final day of the session approached, the students attempted to penetrate military lines set up two kilometers from the MPR. Beatings became more frequent and savage. Students running for cover would be chased and shot with rubber bullets at point blank range.

Though I would have preferred to witness these dramatic events in person, considering both my lack of accreditation and Siti's concern for my safety, I opted to remain in the Kemang Palace during the session. While Heri and other friends kept me informed about the situation on the streets I flipped through the excellent, often live coverage provided by the local channels.

Insulated from the action and the sense of urgency Heri was feeling on the street, and Monica on the Trisakti campus, I watched the proceedings with morbid fascination but no real emotion. I was remote and detached, as though viewing a film. With Siti clutching my arm in terror and frequent interruptions for chat-line commercials, I could have been watching a cheesy Hollywood thriller about a popular independence movement, where anyone in a uniform is an unrepentant murderer and those in torn jeans and headbands are heroic freedom fighters, especially if young and attractive.

Or I could have been watching a quirky, modern movie in which cynical lunacy counterpoints gratuitous violence. During the MPR session, as students were fighting pitched battles with security forces, the worthy members of the sovereign assembly were trying to determine exactly how to cast their votes, never having done so since the establishment of the New Order, when all decisions were taken by mutual agreement, the government persuading recalcitrant representatives to accede to the will of the majority. After hours of confusing deliberation, and reflecting the gravity of the situation, the members chose the failsafe "belt-and-suspenders" route of simultaneously standing and raising their hands.

I believe Habibie shares my enthusiasm for classic Hollywood movies. As the situation deteriorated, with violent incidents in several neighborhoods joining the daily confrontations between military and students, calls mounted to take decisive action. I wondered if Habibie responded as I would in his position, by instructing the police to "round up the usual suspects!"

That would explain the controversial arrests on 12 November. This time, the "usual suspects" were not petty thieves and smugglers but the most respected members of the nation's founding generation, the Angkatan '45. Among them was Ali Sadikin, the Marine general who, during his term as Mayor of Jakarta in the seventies, helped turn a post-colonial backwater into a modern city.

These septuagenarian subversives were arrested for holding a conspiratorial meeting in a luxurious hotel in downtown Jakarta. At this meeting, the purported revolutionaries signed a manifesto demanding the creation—by any and all means—of representative democracy, an independent judiciary, and a free press, as well as immediate cessation of violent acts by all parties. They are also alleged to have distributed inflammatory pamphlets and really delicious coffee and cake to all participants. This final item is the only plausible aspect of whole affair, as I know the hotel's pastry chef is a genius.

On Friday, 13 November, the penultimate day of the MPR session, tensions were running high. Students hurled vicious verbal insults at the soldiers, who often replied with physical assault. Troops would erupt in cheers whenever a demonstrator was clubbed.

Heri was coordinating his group of logistic-support volunteers at the Atma Jaya command post. Trisakti had sent representatives to Atma Jaya, while Monica stayed on campus, charged with keeping communications line open with the group at Atma Jaya.

Heri regarded the troops arrayed near the nearby Semanggi flyover, where he knew the students would be halted, then craned his neck to survey the surrounding rooftops, most of which were twenty stories or more above the street. Heri wondered which glass towers harbored military sharpshooters. Positioned at such a high angle, snipers could pick off targets at will, even inside the campus boundaries. Heri shuddered and continued counting packaged meals.

The demonstration column arrived in mid-afternoon. The front ranks threw rocks at the line of riot police, but no serious attempt was made to break through. Most demonstrators listened to speeches while they had a late lunch. The tension of previous days was not evident. Heri relaxed with the other alumni volunteers, hoping for an early night for the first time in a week.

As dusk approached and the afternoon heat faded, the students made another push to break through the riot line and proceed toward the MPR. Amid the pop of tear-gas canisters, Heri heard the unmistakable staccato crackle of rifle fire. Seconds later, at Trisakti, Monica heard the news as every cell phone in her vicinity began to ring.

"I was so scared the military were going to start killing everyone," Monica told me later. "I thought about going home, but something stopped me. I just felt I was safer here, among my friends."

In fact, fourteen students were killed and scores injured. Seriously wounded demonstrators were rushed to the Jakarta Hospital emergency room only meters away. Less critical cases, including many suffering emotional trauma, were taken to Trisakti. Monica attempted to discover if any Trisakti students were among the injured, so she could inform their families.

She paused in her work long enough to telephone her mother to offer reassurance, her confident voice masking her real feelings.

Monica stayed at her post, keeping communication lines open through the night. Though many Chinese Indonesian students helped out during the day, Monica believed she was the only ethnic Chinese student to remain on campus day and night throughout the MPR session.

When Heri phoned the Kemang Palace later that evening, Siti, Adam, and I were glued to the television, flipping channels in an effort to witness the shocking events from all angles and viewpoints. Heri breathlessly informed me he was holding live shell casings a student had found on the roadway, proof, he claimed, that the Habibie government was no different from the New Order.

Heri explained that the various student activist organizations had devised a plan to burst into the MPR after the close of the session, a sort of replay of the previous May's historic occupation. This time a representative student leader would be declared president, replacing the illegitimate Habibie.

Assuming I had numerous contacts among the foreign journalists, Heri asked me to arrange for the designated "People's President" to be interviewed live on international television. He explained that most of the international journalists were inside the MPR complex, trapped on the other side of the security cordon.

The next day, I made some inquiries among the journalists I knew personally. By this point, with blood running on the streets, none had time for student shenanigans. Two European crews did express interest, asking me to call them when the "People's President" and his entourage was about to storm the MPR.

This was the excuse I had been waiting for. Over Siti's frantic objections, I left the house late Saturday afternoon, convincing an ojek driver to take me downtown. As night fell, we drove through deserted streets to the Atma Jaya University command post, where Heri waited. The driver dropped me off about a hundred meters south of Semanggi, then wheeled around and sped back to the safety of Kemang. I walked under the flyover, hurrying past any soldiers who might ask for my nonexistent press credentials.

I met Heri at Atma Java, then, accompanied by several other alumni support volunteers, we walked along the closed toll road toward the MPR complex. Groups of students and other young men idled on the roadside or sat on guard rails. When they saw me, many would call out greetings and give a thumbs-up gesture of approval.

We stopped a hundred meters short of the riot police line. Rocks and broken glass were scattered between our position and the police line, evidence of the skirmishes a few hours earlier. Heri phoned the University of Indonesia downtown campus every few minutes, trying to ascertain when the convoy of students would embark for the MPR complex. I, in turn, tried telephoning my news-crew contacts. All of them were currently in the neighborhoods near the MPR, where fights had broken out between local residents and Kamra militiamen.

After two hours of waiting, Heri ended his latest call to the student headquarters and looked at me, his face a mask of agonized embarrassment.

"Sorry, Jeremy," he said. "The plan was cancelled. No one is coming."

"What happened? Did someone from the military threaten to shoot them?"

"No," Heri said, sighing. "They could not agree which one of the student leaders would be declared 'President-for-a-Day.'"

Pak Trisno gave a hearty laugh when I told him about the farcical student plan to take over the presidency. He excused himself, and returned a moment later with a wayang puppet of a gangly, long-nosed character he called Petruk.

He described Petruk, one of three servants serving the noble Pandawa Brothers, the "good guys" of the wayang, as one of most influential characters because he has the power of ridicule. Warriors can mock, but they must back up their words with the sword, and can be silenced if they are outnumbered. But Petruk and his brother are under the protection of old Semar, the paunchy, doddering manservant who is actually the most powerful figure in the wayang. Petruk can say anything he wants, but Semar will only reprimand him if he is not respectful to those who genuinely deserve respect, such as a wise and just king or an honest, hardworking farmer.

Pak Trisno showed me the Petruk figure to illustrate one of his favorite wayang episodes: *Petruk Jadi Ratu*, Petruk becomes a king.

"Here we see Petruk as a king with all the accoutrements of royal power," Pak Trisno explained, "but his kingdom is quickly engulfed in chaos, as a clown having real authority disrupts the order of the universe. Because Petruk, you see, is not wise. Like a child, he sees and speaks the truth, mocking the pretentious and exposing the perfidious. But saying how things really are will not automatically make them better."

Muslim Avengers

ON THE NIGHT OF THE "STUDENT PRESIDENT" FIASCO my cell phone probably saved Siti from emotional breakdown. Siti spent the entire evening in front of the television, cell phone in one hand and remote control in the other, flipping through the channels for the latest news. Whenever she saw graphic images of violence she called me to make sure I was still unharmed. After I noticed the "low battery" indicator flashing on my own cell phone I decided to return home immediately to spare Siti the trauma hearing of a "number inactive" automated message when she called again.

With me exhausted from my fruitless journey downtown and Siti physically and emotionally drained from her evening of frenzied channel surfing and telephoning, we retired almost immediately. During the night I was awakened by the sound of a vehicle stopping in front of the Kemang Palace, then voices in rapid, hushed conversation. I was too tired to investigate, trusting Pak Tatang to handle whatever problem had arisen.

When Inem asked permission to return to her home village a few days afterward, I agreed without a second thought. She had appeared nervous and distracted in recent days; I assumed the cause was some family drama. I asked if Darto would be going with her, remembering I had not seen him around for several days. Inem turned away, mumbling a vague reply.

When Inem departed the following day, I was astounded to see Darto emerge from the staff quarters with her, limping and his left arm bandaged. Siti silenced me before I could speak. I watched them walk away, shrugged, and then, as politely as I could manage, asked Siti to explain what the hell was going on.

She, of course, had been fully aware of Darto's clandestine recuperation in the Kemang Palace staff quarters. Siti explained that he had been hanging out with Kamra militia members from his village, hoping to be recruited. During the final night of the MPR session, while I was waiting in vain for the "Student President," Darto and his friends had been involved in one of many altercations between Kamra members and local residents. Siti suspected that the militiamen had abused their paramilitary status by pushing around one of the locals.

Darto had suffered parang gashes on his arm and an injured ankle. After Marine Corps troops arrived to restore order, Darto had been taken to a nearby military hospital to be patched up, then driven to the Kemang Palace. Afraid of my reaction—knowing I regarded Darto as nothing more than a preman—Siti, Inem, Pak Tatang, and Uus conspired to keep me unaware of his presence until Inem could take him back to Central Java.

If I believed Darto's departure would restore tranquility to the Kemang Palace, I was sadly mistaken. I had neglected to consider Adam's systematic alienation of the entire neighborhood as well as his chronic absentmindedness, both of which put the Kemang Palace in frequent jeopardy. Some mornings Pak Tatang would find the gate unlocked and Adam's keys hanging from the front door latch, left there forgotten when he returned, groggy and distracted, from a late-night rehearsal.

Worse, Adam would leave his keys in the back seat of his taxi, which meant an unknown number of taxi drivers knew the house and had a copy of the gate and door keys. When repeated admonitions to pay greater attention to security had no effect, I reminded Adam that Javanese etiquette required he lay out tea and a snack in the reception area before retiring, considering he had issued an open invitation for burglars to visit. At any rate, I had to change the locks so often the neighborhood locksmith's wife sent me a cake in appreciation of the steady business.

More worrisome yet were the frequent fights between Adam and taxi and ojek drivers. At least twice a week a taxi would pull up to the gate, followed by voices raised in heated argument over the amount of change Adam received, or Adam's refusal to pay the entire meter amount because the driver had not taken the most direct route, though in Jakarta's unpredictable traffic detours can save time by avoiding bottlenecks. I cautioned Adam about making a fuss over literally pennies, to no avail. He thought that drivers were lucky to have a job during Krismon; they should not abuse their good fortune by fleecing foreign passengers.

Late one evening I heard a motorcycle stop in front of the house, then voices raised in anger. The motorcycle sped away, making an unnecessary amount of noise in the process. Adam entered, muttering about the ojek driver wanting ten thousand rupiah for a two-kilometer ride. I reminded Adam ojek fares tend to go up at night—especially for a bule in Kemang.

A few minutes later, I heard the piercing racket of massed small motorcycle engines. I stepped onto the second-floor balcony and saw about a dozen motorcycles approaching the Kemang Palace. I recognized many of the riders as ojek drivers from seeing them lounging at their gathering point down the street.

As in a scene in a biker movie, the ojek drivers gathered in front of the house, revving their engines and playing their headlights over the walls. Adam, Siti, and I were alone. The other houses in the cul-de-sac were still unoccupied, and the block's night watchman, who knew all the ojek drivers, had chosen that moment to buy cigarettes at the warung in the adjoining block.

I discovered later that the driver was fully justified in demanding a surcharge. Adam had been attending a rehearsal at a fellow gamelan aficionado's home in a neighborhood adjacent to Kemang. At rehearsal's end, Adam's host had sent a servant to summon an ojek for his guest, but Adam had kept the driver waiting while he conversed with his fellow gamelan players. In addition, when Adam was halfway home he realized he left his glasses at the rehearsal venue. Adam ordered the driver to return for the lost article before continuing home. In all, the driver was occupied for almost an hour.

Siti scanned down the list of public-service telephone numbers posted beside the telephone, then dialed the police rapid-response unit number. When no one answered the telephone she slammed down the handset, muttering imprecations at the Indonesian police. She vented her frustration on Adam, castigating him for his penny-pinching stupidity, the first words she had spoken to him in a month. Adam did not protest, perhaps belatedly realizing he was to blame for our predicament.

I wanted to talk with the ojek drivers, but Siti urged me not to go outside. We were at a standoff when Pak Tatang and Uus arrived from a late evening prayer meeting at the local mosque. Pak Tatang, dressed in a sarong, *baju koko* embroidered jacket, a woven prayer shawl draped over his right shoulder, and a black, rimless *peci* on his head cut an incongruous but dignified figure in the midst of the denim-clad bikers, who ceased shouting and revving their engines when he approached. I called to Pak Tatang and explained the situation briefly, which elicited another round of noisemaking from the drivers. Siti squeezed my arm with one hand and bit the nails of the other.

Pak Tatang asked us to remain calm, then turned to the aggrieved ojek driver. After listening to the driver's voluble complaints, he reached to his hip pocket for his wallet, then smiled when he realized he was wearing a sarong. He took his gate keys from the breast pocket of his baju koko, hesitated, replaced the keys and checked the two side pockets of his baju, and found a few one-thousand rupiah notes. Pak Tatang gave all the money to the driver, who protested the amount, but Pak Tatang only shrugged his shoulders in helpless apology. Still grumbling, the driver accepted the money.

I silently praised Pak Tatang for having the presence of mind not to open the front gate while emotions were running high. He motioned for all the drivers to disperse. As they drove away, again revving their machines more than strictly necessary, Pak Tatang unlocked the front gate and entered the house.

We all descended from the second floor and went to the staff quarters. As I thanked Pak Tatang for handling the situation, he listened with an expectant expression. I realized that he was too polite to ask himself, so I reminded Adam to reimburse Pak Tatang for the money he had given the ojek driver. Adam, still shaken, fumbled in his wallet. He extracted a brand-new fifty thousand rupiah note, handing it to Pak Tatang while saying how much he appreciated his assistance. I smiled, remembering the numerous occasions Adam had accused Pak Tatang of petty embezzlement and his general disregard for the old man.

Pak Tatang regarded the crisp new note for a moment, then gave it back to Adam.

"Don't you have anything smaller, Mr. Adam?" he said. "You only owe me four thousand rupiah."

A few days after the incident with the Kemang chapter of the Hell's Angels I returned home at nightfall and entered the bedroom to discover Siti, wearing a pink, body-concealing robe and headdress, kneeling on a small rug performing sunset prayers. I always feel uncomfortable barging in on a private prayer session, so I mumbled an apology and left the room. Though I was hot, exhausted, and craving a cold beer, my usual sundowner on the back terrace somehow seemed inappropriate at that moment. I waited outside the door and pondered Siti's sudden, unexpected onset of piety.

During all my years in Indonesia, I had had little direct contact with Islam, the religion professed by about ninety percent of the population. For me, Islam was only one element of the picturesque Indonesian backdrop. I enjoyed observing the solemn dignity of communal worship and hearing the hauntingly beautiful call for prayer from a village mosque silhouetted against a blood-red sunset. Less aesthetically pleasing was the screeching cacophony of a local youth with admirable conviction and a total lack of voice control bellowing through an overdriven mosque public address system an hour before sunrise. However, in general the architecture, practices, and moral influence of the Way of the Prophet make a significant and welcome contribution to the archipelago's charm.

Islam also did not figure prominently in the life of my former family or any of my close Indonesian friends. My first wife, a Christian from an island in the eastern end of the Indonesian archipelago, combined a disparaging view of Islam with her general contempt for all things Javanese. I remember her being near apoplexy one Friday when our six-year-old son donned a sarong and announced he was going to the neighborhood mosque with his playmates.

Farid, though nominally a Muslim, is the black sheep of his devout mercantile family from Java's north coast. Farid claims, tongue-in-cheek, that he stopped practicing Islam as a teenager when he realized he would never be good at it. In fact, while Farid has seldom seen the inside of a mosque, in many important respects he lives an exemplary life by Islamic standards. Farid does not drink or gamble, has read the Koran, and generously supports community social services and activities. On the other hand, whenever I visit his command center in the early morning to watch some special sports or news event on a satellite channel he cooks us what he calls an "apostate's breakfast," otherwise known as bacon and eggs.

During the first months of our relationship, Siti's behavior, notably her fondness for margaritas, indicated, at best, a nominal adherence to Islam. At a shopping mall or other public area both Siti and I would make humorously disparaging comments about "*jilbab* girls," teenagers sporting Muslim dress—which leaves only face and hands exposed—while shopping or hanging out in trendy caf s. When Siti began to observe Islamic practices seriously, I realized her contempt for "jilbab girls" was actually a condemnation of their hypocrisy in outwardly conforming to Islamic precepts of public modesty while indulging in conspicuous consumption and social-status competition, such as dating when barely into their teens.

I noticed Siti was frequently in the staff quarters, discussing Islam with Pak Tatang and Uus, as well as reading booklets explaining the proper observance of Islam's bewildering canon of rules and regulations. One day I entered the staff quarters looking for Siti, thinking she might be having an impromptu session of religious instruction with Pak Tatang. Instead I stumbled onto Uus trying on an impressive all-white costume, complete with a dashing waist-band and turban. He was embarrassed to be discovered, quickly explaining his costume was for special prayer sessions at the mosque during the upcoming holy month of Ramadan. Later, when I told Siti about Uus's flashy Arab-style gear, she joked he had probably joined a *jihad* gang.

I was not amused. Youthful experiences with leftist politics and fundamentalist religious groups left me with a deep-seated fear and loathing of extremism in any form. I asked Pak Trisno if he knew the reasons behind the new phenomenon of militant Islam organizations, the jihad gangs.

"It's obvious," he replied. "Many Indonesian Muslims feel Islam is facing a grave threat."

This was news to me; Indonesia has the largest Muslim population in the world. Pak Trisno admitted this was correct, but likened calling Indonesia a Muslim nation to describing Europe as a Christian continent. Though accurate in the broadest sense, the term glosses over enormous variations in custom, belief, and personal commitment to the religion.

Unfortunately, as Pak Trisno pointed out, in Indonesia religious groupings often tend to correspond with social divisions. The superior educational opportunities afforded by the foreign-funded mission schools during the late colonial period and early years of nationhood resulted in a disproportionate number of Christians in the top ranks of government, military, and business. Closer to the grass-roots level, Chinese Indonesians who chose not to adhere to Buddhism usually adopted Christianity.

Social activists had exploited this polarization for years, embracing Islam with a degree of sincerity directly proportionate to their scruples. In the current crisis, religious leaders had no trouble convincing the disaffected, frustrated, and just-plain-hungry that their misery was rooted in a wide-spread assault on Islam.

"Hard times make people look for easy answers," Pak Trisno said, "and religious fundamentalism, is, as you Americans might say, a 'no-brainer.' I suggest you be careful when you go out of the house."

I did not think further about Uus of Arabia until the following Sunday, when, returning home from a wedding reception with Siti, I overheard the fleet radio dispatcher warning all drivers to avoid the Ketapang area in Central Jakarta, where a riot was in progress.

Arriving home, we turned on the television in time to view scenes of a building in flames, identified as the Ketapang Church. I was shocked. I had a connection with the church through Stephanie, a client who was active in church-sponsored social work. Stephanie had recently asked me to write the narration for a video her production house was making to raise funds for missionary programs in Irian Jaya, the Indonesian portion of New Guinea. When I telephoned her several hours later, Stephanie put me in contact with Pak Sadiman, a church employee who had witnessed the incident.

Ketapang is a multi-ethnic warren of shop houses and kampung-style dwellings enclosed by major commercial avenues. According to Sadiman, whose version was later confirmed by other eyewitness accounts, the incident began late the previous evening with a fight between the doorman of a gambling parlor next door to the church and the driver of a *bajaj*, a three-wheeled vehicle widely used for short distance transport in the area. The driver was a Javanese Muslim and the doorman a Christian from the island of Ambon. The Ambonese, who regard beer drinking and friendly card games as traditional cultural pursuits, operate most the entertainment centers in Ketapang.

Word of the altercation, soon embellished by a rumor that a group of Ambonese had vandalized a local mosque, spread through Ketapang's crowded alleyways during the night. On Sunday morning, a crowd gathered near the entertainment center, which is adjacent to the Ketapang church. At eight a.m., when the early morning service ended, the predominantly Chinese congregation were able to leave without incident, though the crowd now filled the street in front of the church. Several church officers and members remained to prepare for the second service.

No one appeared for the second service. Those who had remained inside the church debated the best course of action until ten thirty, when a stone flew through a plate-glass window and the mob forced open the front gate. Because of the high walls surrounding the premises, the only way out was through the midst of the crowd now spilling into the parking lot. All suffered verbal abuse and most women had their handbags snatched out of their arms as they passed through the mob. One young minister was beaten and chased down the street, but managed to scramble over a wall and escape through the back alleyways.

Sadiman, a church employee who was the only pribumi in the church that day, chose to remain at the scene. He watched the unfolding events from a restaurant across the road, which was safe from attack because several armed soldiers stood at the entrance, thanks to the owner's close connections with the army.

Sadiman told me he saw white-robed figures, some waving green Islamic flags, goading on the rioters. Others took cans of kerosene from roadside warung and carried them into the church building. In minutes, the entire structure was in flames.

By the end of the afternoon, the mobs had burned fourteen churches in Ketapang and surrounding areas, and had hacked or stoned to death several Christians, including the unfortunate doorman. Indonesian Islam had shown an ugly—and so far hidden—face to the world.

Where's the Chicken?

THE MOOD IN JAKARTA SHIFTED DRAMATICALLY after the Semanggi shootings and Ketapang riot. Taxi drivers, those unerring barometers of social disposition, became staunch supporters of the students they had previously denounced as spoiled brats. Most drivers resigned themselves to the daily traffic gridlock caused by the student demonstrations, though the hours of immobility cut deeply into their earnings.

"It's like strong medicine," one driver told me. "It may taste bad, but if you don't take it, you will never get well."

The students were administering their version of cod liver oil to the body politic in increasing doses. Most felt the demise of their fourteen fellow students at Semanggi belied the purported efforts of the MPR to create a framework for true democracy. The students' stated goal was now the immediate, total eradication of all vestiges of the New Order.

During the weeks after Semanggi, Monica neglected her studies to devote all of her time to the student movement. While she did her share of support work at the campus, she was often in the field, documenting rallies and other events as her committee's unofficial photographer.

Ketapang is only a few kilometers from the Trisakti campus. The day after the riot, the Trisakti student committee decided to do some freelance investigation of the riot scene, specifically to discover possible evidence of New Order involvement in the incident. Monica's own home lies between Ketapang and Trisakti. She tried to suppress images of her own neighborhood in ruins as she photographed the smashed shop windows, the coils of barbed wire around Gajah Mada Plaza, the burnt-out shell of the Ketapang church, and a patch of dried blood near a drain.

During the reform era, the term "Little Soehartos" had come into vogue to describe, among other things, the propensity of student organizers to indulge in a little authortarianism of their own. During the final days of the MPR occupation, for example, Monica was rebuffed when she tried to gain access to the top floor of one building to take a high-angle photograph of the MPR grounds. She later learned students had been ransacking offices and destroying government files. Now, in Ketapang, she noticed her colleagues acting in the same imperious manner as they questioned pedestrians and stopped passing automobiles to interrogate their occupants.

When Monica's companions halted one late-model luxury sedan carrying several Chinese passengers, they called to her to take photographs. While the driver was engrossed in conversation with his interrogators, Monica photographed those in the back seat. She adjusted her Polaroid filter to remove the window glare, revealing the face of a middle-aged Chinese woman, who stared at Monica with a quizzical, then disapproving expression. Monica lowered her camera, suddenly aware of her incongruous situation as a

Chinese woman documenting the questioning, bordering on harassment, of her ethnic fellows. Monica backed away from the vehicle began photographing the damage to shops and other buildings.

As the "Little Soehartos" were making pests of themselves, their namesake was back in the news as the focus of investigations into New Order corruption. Two months previously, Soeharto had made his first public appearance since his resignation. The jovial leader had appeared regularly on television during his years in power, pre-empting programming on all stations after the evening news. When not opening a factory or toll road, he was engaged in conversations with common Indonesians in carefully stage-managed but often spontaneous and entertaining sessions. He offered sound and practical advice on farming and other earthy matters. Though ill-at-ease around foreign dignitaries and meek and self-depreciatory when faced with the Javanese aristocracy, Soeharto was his own man among the people.

On this occasion, he had used an hour of prime time on his daughter's television station to assure the nation "he is not a crook." Soeharto carefully explained he did not have billions stashed away in a Swiss bank. This was probably true, as several weeks earlier an agency in the US Treasury Department charged with monitoring large international transactions had reported a mysterious multi-billion-dollar transfer of funds from a bank in Switzerland to a similar institution in Austria. A few days after his television appearance, Soeharto presented himself in person at the attorney general's office, and graciously granted permission for a full probe into his financial affairs.

After weeks of probing revealed nothing, Attorney General Ghalib responded to criticism by claiming "to catch a chicken thief, you must first produce the chicken." The following day, Monica photographed students presenting Ghalib with a hen—itself a humiliating symbolic insult for the Bugis of South Sulawesi, Ghalib's ethnic group. When asked about the chicken at a subsequent cabinet meeting, Ghalib replied the chicken was slaughtered and eaten by his staff.

"Presumably destroying the evidence," a voice was heard to say.

When I discussed the chicken incident with Pak Trisno, I was surprised to hear him criticise the search for Soeharto's legendary billions, believing it to be a vendetta rather than a search for justice.

"Until he dies," Pak Trisno said, "and maybe afterward as well, Indonesians will scream for Soeharto's head on a platter."

"Why not?" I countered. "Corruption is responsible for Krismon and all the political chaos we have suffered since."

"Your exceptional talent for oversimplification is of little use here, my friend," Pak Trisno said. "Corruption, in one form or another, is as much a part of Indonesian life as rice."

According to Pak Trisno, Soeharto had used corruption as Soekarno had used oratory, as a instrument to wield political power. Just as Soekarno's rousing rhetoric eventually proved inappropriate to address the grave problems Indonesia faced in the sixties, Soeharto's patronage and reward system worked well for years, then ran out of control as the economy grew and countless opportunities for corruption were created.

"You must remember," he continued, "Soeharto ascended to the presidency of a nation in disintegration. The economy was barely functioning, the political elite was spending all their time and energy jockeying for power, and outlying regions were again edging toward open rebellion."

According to Pak Trisno, Soeharto's solution was to rebuild the government from the ground up. Though outwardly a modern democracy, Soeharto's Indonesia more resembled the great Javanese empires of the past. Like an ancient sultan doling out largesse, Soeharto used the money flooding in from foreign investors exploiting Indonesia's petroleum reserves, forests, and other natural resources to award positions, commercial monopolies, and outright cash to senior military officers, relatives, trusted friends, and potential enemies.

"But that money wasn't his," I said. "It belonged to all the Indonesian people."

"Maybe so, but since ancient times the king has physically possessed and controlled all the wealth of the kingdom. Soeharto felt it was his right to use that money."

"What about the common people? They deserved money more than anyone."

"Soeharto's largesse was not a gift, it was a payment to ensure future loyalty."

"How could he be sure? Some might just take the money and run."

"A common coolie maybe, but not a man of position. Once he has entered the great money stream

controlled by the president, he acquires countless
financial obligations of his own: to family,
subordinates, and the community. He cannot afford
to have his income cut off. Though the recipient will
claim he is keeping up his side of the agreement
through a sense of honor and humble recognition of
his position, he also knows what is bestowed by the
king can be just as easily taken away."

I nodded thoughtfully. His argument made sense,
but Pak Trisno's take on the former dictator seemed
strange considering his own terrible experiences.

"You seem remarkably sympathetic toward a man
who kept you in prison for years," I said, trying not
to sound too skeptical.

"I can't blame Soeharto personally for my fate. He
did what he thought was right. Besides, I knew him. I
thought he was, as you might say, 'a great guy.' He
was unfailingly polite and even charming in a subdued
and distant way."

My jaw dropped. Pak Trisno waited for my mouth
to close again before proceeding.

"I met Soeharto in the early sixties, at the shipyard
owned by my friend Mochtar, whom I often visited
during my journalist days. He was a good source, being
privy to all the gossip of the harbor, particularly who
was smuggling what.

"Then head of Kostrad, Soeharto came to the
shipyard to inspect the prototype of a coastal patrol
boat Mochtar was offering to build. Mochtar, myself,
Suharto, and Ibu Tien with little Tommy on her hip
took the prototype out for a demonstration run in the
harbor. After a few minutes, Soeharto insisted on
taking the wheel. He was obviously a land army man,

because we careened alarmingly for a few minutes before he ran us right into a sandbar. As Mochtar leapt to the rear to shut down the engine, Soeharto turned around, beaming, saying he would take a dozen of the craft."

I laughed, saying Soeharto running the boat onto a sandbar was an apt metaphor for what he did to the nation in subsequent years.

"Not exactly," Pak Trisno replied. "The incident would have been an uncanny foreshadowing of later events only if Soeharto had insisted his wife become a partner in the shipyard and the first boat be given to little Tommy as a toy."

During the rest of November I continued my efforts to acquire some sort of accreditation from Deppen. Though I had little intention of pursuing journalistic activities, I knew that in Indonesia, as in most countries with a large, well-entrenched bureaucracy, one can never have too many permits, licenses, or other official documents. Like a protective magic ring or amulet, a press card could be used to ward off extortion attempts and other petty annoyances with the implicit threat of exposing the perpetrator.

I haunted the Department of Information hallways during my free afternoons. Passed from desk to desk like an unwanted and potentially damaging document, I came to feel sorry for many of these career bureaucrats. Their greatest fear is making a mistake, so they scrupulously follow the rules. But when the rules change daily, as at Deppen during the reform era, they must feel as though their scuffed office floors are heaving and buckling under their feet.

I assumed that part of the problem was that I had yet to pay any sort of "administration fee." I dare not broach the subject myself. I waited to be asked, so I could negotiate a fair price. I expected Pak Adé, my primary contact person, to initiate the process through a hint or oblique reference, but when we met he seemed happy just to chat with me about the changes at Deppen.

This reluctance to solicit money to process my admittedly extraordinary request was the more puzzling considering Pak Adé's background. I never discovered his precise official rank in the Deppen bureaucracy, but through his own comments and information supplied by Farid and others, I realized that his primary—but wholly unofficial—duty during previous years had been to function as a "bag man."

Pak Adé never saw the serious money flowing into the upper echelons of Deppen. As in other government departments and state-owned corporations, top Deppen officials secured shareholdings and directorships in companies falling under their jurisdiction, generating the funds needed to finance palatial mansions, luxury automobiles, lavish weddings, international shopping sprees, and other examples of egregious corruption.

On the other hand, Pak Adé ran the traditional corruption machine found in all government offices. He collected "administration fees" and other routine payments from print publications for fair and equitable distribution among all employees in his department, from division managers to office boys. Without Pak Adé's monthly envelopes supplementing their meager official salary, few civil servants could survive, much less raise families.

Civil servants describe the various postings in government service as "wet" or "dry," depending on how much opportunity each position affords to supplement official income through illegal levees, commissions on goods procurement, and other corrupt practises. During the New Order, most positions in Deppen had been fairly damp. However, in the months since the change in government, as Deppen's control over the Indonesian media was reduced and finally eliminated, the once-powerful department had become a corruption desert, and Pak Adé was sitting atop the highest and driest sand dune.

Pak Adé had been relegated to *surga pegawai negeri*, civil servant heaven. Though still holding a high rank, he had no staff, no budget, no programs, nothing to do but wait for retirement. Normally, denizens of *surga pegawai negeri* concentrate on managing their outside interests. But Pak Adé had never developed the usual shadow business empire. His one source of outside income was a partnership in a small printing house, now on the verge of bankruptcy because of the drop in revenue combined with the rising cost of paper, ink, and other imported materials.

As Krismon continued, demands for assistance increased in inverse proportion to Pak Adé's dwindling income. Previously unknown relatives appeared, pleading for help in paying medical bills, school fees, even to buy enough rice to make it through Ramadan and the Idul Fitri holiday season.

Pak Adé was in no position to assist anyone. Without his share of the corruption cash flow, Pak Adé only had his seven hundred thousand rupiah official salary, at the time about a hundred dollars. Compared to the demands on his resources, this was pocket change. Pak Adé could barely feed his immediate family; assistance to others was out of the question. Worsening nutrition and hygiene during Krismon was raising the prevalence of serious contagious diseases like dengue fever and typhoid, which can be fatal if not treated properly. Whenever he refused to pay for medical treatment for yet another distant relative or neighbor, Pak Adé could not shake the feeling that he might be condemning the unsuccessful supplicant to death just because he could no longer reach into his wallet and pull out a few million rupiah.

If I had been a *bule kere*, Pak Adé was in a much more untenable position. Accustomed to a lifetime sinecure, where he could be relied upon to fulfill his familial and social obligations, he had become a *bapak kere*, perhaps the worst possible loss of face for an Indonesian.

During one prior visit, Pak Adé had asked a favor. He was compelled to sell—or at least rent—his house in Bali, and he asked if I knew any foreigners who wanted a charming, Balinese-style house in the rice fields. Through Pak Trisno I contacted Woulter, a Dutch furniture trader who was considering a permanent move to Bali. Woulter telephoned me a few days afterward to tell me he had seen the house and wanted more information about ownership of the land. He told me he would not deal directly with Balinese landowners, having heard the horror stories of foreigners buying the usage rights for land from the assumed owner—only an Indonesian citizen can hold freehold title—then being confronted by brothers and other relatives with equally valid claims to ownership. I gave him Pak Adé's contact information and suggested he offer to rent for a year with an option to buy land usage rights for thirty years, if and when Pak Adé provided incontrovertible proof of sole ownership.

While visiting Deppen the following week, Pak Adé thanked me for my efforts, saying he had made a satisfactory arrangement with Woulter. He then reached into a desk drawer, took out an envelope, and handed it to me, explaining it contained one million rupiah, my commission for arranging the deal. Stunned, I took the envelope from Pak Adé's hand and mumbled a few words of appreciation, all the while thinking how bizarre it was to be accepting an envelope full of cash from a civil servant, instead of the other way around. I wondered if the labyrinthine path I had taken through the Deppen building had brought me into a parallel universe, where normal actions are reversed, like a film running backward.

Pulang Kampung

THE NEXT DAY AT THE KEMANG PALACE, I heard the unprecedented and disturbing sound of Pak Tatang's voice raised in anger. I had learned to stay out of staff disputes, but since Pak Tatang seemed genuinely angry, and his voice was disturbing my concentration when I was struggling to meet a tight deadline, I decided to investigate.

I found Pak Tatang sitting in his favorite chair, chastising Uus, who was squatting, head bowed, on the floor beside him. When I asked Pak Tatang what the problem was, the old man only continued his tirade.

"Those people aren't Muslims," he said. "*Orang Islam bukan tukang pukul.*" Muslims are not head bashers.

Pak Tatang explained he had learned through a friend at the mosque that Uus was attending meetings of an Islamic extremist group. Though Uus was adamant he had not taken part in the Ketapang Riot, Pak Tatang believed it was only a matter of time before Uus became involved in a vigilante incident of some sort. Already, some groups were threatening to raid nightclubs and other dens of iniquity, to purge the city of sin before the coming Ramadan fasting month.

Pak Tatang asked permission to take Uus back to their village the following morning, several days before his regular end-of-the-month trip. I agreed and paid his salary early, with a bonus for Uus's bus fare.

Adam was furious when I told him of Pak Tatang's early departure. Without telling Siti or me, Adam had scheduled a dress rehearsal for the upcoming televised wayang performance. With Inem gone, he needed Pak Tatang to shop for the required drinks and snacks, and to serve them to his guests throughout the rehearsal, which would probably extend past midnight.

I was going to grumble about Adam's lack of consideration, then checked myself. Adam was under a lot of stress. His planned performance with the dalang had been postponed almost a month because of the social unrest. With the dalang fully booked for the month of Ramadan, he could only schedule the performance for the following week.

I found myself apologizing for letting Pak Tatang leave early. Adam walked around our cul-de-sac, looking for other house watchers who might be willing to help. He found them all playing dominoes in one garage. No one wanted the extra work, being too involved in the game and believing that serving snacks was beneath their dignity. At a loss, I suggested he ask Siti for help when she returned home.

As he begged Siti for assistance, I saw genuine anguish. Not serving drinks and snacks to his guests would be an inexcusable breach of manners, especially since he was asking his musicians to undergo considerable inconvenience. The gamelan members, like most Jakartans, were reluctant to leave their homes during the evening because of the continuing unrest.

When Siti saw the distress in Adam's face, all

animosity evaporated. Though she still held her housemate in a fair degree of contempt, she could not let him run the risk of being considered *kurang ajar*— under-educated or not-quite-Javanese—for neglecting his duties as host. Adam went to his room to get money for the coffee, soft drinks, sweet cakes, and fried bananas, but typically had difficulty finding his wallet. Siti told him not to bother, she would be happy to help out. Adam thanked her, and Siti came upstairs to ask me for twenty thousand rupiah.

The dalang was one of the first to arrive for the rehearsal. Never having met an authentic dalang, I had expected a Javanese gentleman of overwhelming formality and priestly manners, steeped in ancient philosophy, the epitome of all things Javanese. I was surprised to meet a lively figure with a ready wit and easy laugh. Though a few minutes' conversation demonstrated he possessed all the emotional restraint and formidable courtesy of a Javanese aristocrat, he also had the earthy spontaneity of a showman equally at home performing in a formal theater or a village square. Siti blossomed under his charm, the first time I had seen her react favorably to an Indonesian male.

As expected, a student demonstration prevented several gamelan members from attending. Adam swapped positions as best he could, but one set of gongs lacked a player. Since this particular position involved no more than keeping a simple rhythm, following the lead of other players, the dalang suggested Adam ask Siti for assistance.

The dalang correctly assumed that Siti, like most young Indonesians, had learned to play simple gamelan tunes at some point during her schooling. Later on, I looked downstairs to see Siti, in sarong and T-shirt, her long hair tied in a *konde*, the traditional Javanese woman's hairstyle, and face set in fierce concentration as she struck the sonorous bronze gongs.

In Indonesia, divorce is seldom a life-shattering event. While some Indonesian ethnic groups—and, of course, the nation's Catholic population—officially adhere to a once-in-a-lifetime marriage policy, many Indonesians marry and divorce with unseemly alacrity. Nevertheless, I was astounded when Heri phoned one day to tell me that Yani had taken Satria and moved in with her mother.

I met Yani for coffee at the first opportunity. She was eager to talk, perhaps because she needed to explain her case to someone impartial. She told me her problems with Heri began the morning Yani's mother called with an opportunity to supplement the family income. Since the MPR had set the date for the new general election, and lifted the New Order restrictions on political organizations, political parties had replaced BMWs as status symbols for the elite. Yani's mother was receiving numerous invitations from long-time admirers to sing at political fund-raising events. She rejected these offers, but thought Yani, who she had taught to sing at an early age, might be interested. To her astonishment, Heri refused even to consider his wife singing in public for any reason.

"I was so surprised I forgot to get angry," Yani complained. "This was not the man I married."

According to Yani, they had begun married life as a modern, urban couple. Instead of the traditional Indonesian reception ceremony, where bride and groom sit on a pair of thrones—literally king and queen for

a day—Heri and Yani invited their friends and relatives
to a simple party with wine and karaoke. Heri refused
to consider the usual newlywed arrangement of living
with one or another's parents. They rented a tiny house
in a lower-middle-class neighborhood, like a young
western couple in a one-bedroom apartment.

Yani noticed subtle but unmistakable changes in
Heri's attitude after he joined the bank. Though he
spent many evenings working late or being entertained
by bank clients, he would discourage Yani from
socializing with her own friends, even a girl's night
out with other Indoyup wives. According to Heri, it
was unseemly for the wife of a bank executive to be
seen in nightspots without her husband.

Considering Heri's business associates included
conservative Indonesians such as religious leaders and
government officials, Yani accepted her husband's
concerns as reasonable. But she was growing bored.
The year before Krismon, a college classmate had asked
Yani to join his newly established public relations firm.
Heri told her to turn down the job. According to him,
PR women—often former models or movie stars—are
popularly believed to offer sexual services to their clients.

I tried to hide a smile so as not to offend Yani.

"Now it is not just boredom or appearances," Yani
said. "We really need the money. I feel like I have gone
to bed with a modern Indonesian man and woken up
the next morning with Pak Haji from the kampung."

Yani insisted Heri's continuing unemployment was
not the problem. One of the more dismal trends to
emerge during Krismon was a steep jump in the divorce
rate. Thousands of husbands who, through no fault of
their own, could no longer support their families were
summarily jettisoned as excess baggage.

Yani still loved Heri. In view of Heri's growing conservatism and intransigence, she had been forced to chose between obeying her husband or guaranteeing sufficient cash reserves for her family in this time of crisis. I asked Yani if she might seek reconciliation if Heri started working again. She shook her head.

"We would only go back to the old life. We would have to drive a new BMW, eat in chic cafés, and throw lavish parties. Most likely Heri would force me to give up my sales work. At most, he might set me up in a gift shop or some other respectable business to keep me busy."

Yani's expression told me her days as an Indoyup wife were over regardless of Heri's employment situation.

I was anxious to hear Heri's side of the story, so I jumped at an invitation for afternoon coffee at his house. Yani had taken only personal items for her and Satria, leaving the rest of their property with Heri— including the espresso machine. As we enjoyed our cappuccino on the front terrace, I asked Heri how he was adapting to single life. Heri was coping. Yani permitted him unlimited assess to Satria, who enjoyed his new life. He adored his grandmother, and every time Heri appeared was a special occasion, an excuse to go out for hamburgers.

Heri and Yani had also decided against trying to dispose of the house in the Krismon property market, where suburban bungalows changed hands for US$10,000. To avoid losing the house in a debt default Heri called in an outstanding favor from the supervisor of the lending bank's data processing department, to ensure his name was not flagged for missed payments. Like the highest-ranking directors of Indonesia's sprawling, bankrupt conglomerates, Heri, at least until a comprehensive audit, enjoyed immunity from asset seizure.

However, he could no longer rely on Yani's income to meet his living expenses. When I asked how he intended to survive, Heri beckoned me to follow him through the house and into the back yard, which was filled with covered wooden boxes on meter-high platforms. He lifted the cover from one box, reached inside and pulled out a wriggling handful of worms and soil.

Heri had become a worm farmer. When I told him he should be wearing a Javanese farmer's traditional *lurik* rough-weave shirt and straw hat, Heri laughed and explained worm farming is actually a scientific operation requiring close attention to soil conditions and nutrients. I asked who, besides fishermen, were his customers. Heri reeled off a list of applications in the cosmetics and pharmaceuticals industries. He was also using e-mail to interest overseas buyers in Indonesian earthworms.

Returning inside, Heri expounded his new passion for developing small and medium enterprises, or SMEs. He believed small-scale, labor-intensive operations like his worm farm, as long as they employed modern quality-control practices, were the nation's salvation.

"With the large corporations bankrupt or in foreign hands, small business is Indonesia's road back to prosperity."

Christmas in Ketapang

ONE AFTERNOON IN EARLY DECEMBER, Monica's documentation of the students' struggle to keep the reform movement on track took her to the Hotel Indonesia roundabout in Central Jakarta, where hundreds of female students were protesting a call by the Minister of Women's Affairs to remain in class like good girls instead of joining their male colleagues in the continuing round of disruptive public demonstrations. The police, perhaps assuming this assignment was their version of "women's work," had dispatched members of the *polwan*, the women's police auxiliary, to control the crowd and maintain traffic flow through this strategic downtown intersection.

If an inherent gallantry had inhibited male riot police from pummeling and manhandling female demonstrators on previous occasions, the *polwan* were under no such cultural restraints. As stocky policewomen wrestled with willowy students, the orderly demonstration deteriorated into a mêlée. Monica's camera and Chinese features drew special attention; she sought safety by sticking close to a pack of foreign journalists.

A few days afterward, Monica was at the Atma Jaya campus, photographing student organization representatives who had been physically abused at the nearby police headquarters. Monica was astounded to discover that the students had not been dragged off the street but had gone to the headquarters on their own initiative to meet with police and explore possibilities for reconciliation.

The accounts of these incidents, suitably embellished as they spread through the student movement, sparked off a heated debate between those insisting the demonstrations must remain peaceful to be effective, versus more militant leaders demanding violence be met with violence.

The militants won the argument when students marching toward the MPR complex were halted at the Taman Ria overpass, about one kilometer from their destination. This time students hurled more than slogans and insults at the phalanx of riot police. A flurry of stone throwing and a few Molotov cocktails lobbed at their feet sent the incompetently commanded troops into a disorderly retreat, pursued by demonstrators bellowing in victory.

Ahead on points, the students called for a time out to observe the Islamic holy month of Ramadan, when the faithful must refrain from eating or drinking from dawn to dusk. While the mutually accepted rationale for the cessation in hostilities was the religious directive to avoid confrontation and seek spiritual peace during the holy month, I suspect both students and soldiers dreaded the prospect of hours in the tropical afternoon sun without a drop of water—a rigorous test of both political zeal and military discipline.

At any rate, the entire nation seems to gear down during the fasting month. While fasting can be soothing nourishment for the soul, the month-long round of daytime abstention and nocturnal gorging plays merry havoc with the body's blood-sugar balance. With no recourse to coffee or cigarettes to alleviate midday hunger pangs and provide an emergency energy boost, most people choose to sleep through the hot afternoon. Activity shifts to the nighttime hours, as the futility of retiring in the evening only to rise a few hours later for the substantial pre-dawn breakfast encourages remaining awake to attend family or community events such as prayer sessions or cultural performances.

Indonesia, unlike many countries with large Muslim populations, does not compel Muslim citizens to observe Ramadan. No religious police burst into private homes during the daytime hours to arrest a wretched backslider cowering in a corner with a plate of rice. Such overt coercion is neither desired nor necessary. A disapproving gaze from a family member or friend is enough to ensure strict adherence to Ramadan religious injunctions—most of the time.

While non-Muslims are not obliged to fast, no one —pious pribumi or foreign infidel—is exempt from participating in the round of Ramadan fast-breaking gatherings. Though I tried to beg off, Siti insisted I attend a family gathering at her Aunt Emma's house, where most of Siti's mother's sizable extended family was assembling on the first evening of Ramadan—an especially holy occasion—to pray for a speedy resolution to the multiple crises plaguing their nation.

After breaking fast with an assortment of sweet cakes and *kolak*, a delectable concoction of coconut milk, palm sugar, and bananas which is my favorite Ramadan treat, the family prepared for all-night prayers. The spacious living room had been cleared and an exquisitely carved wooden divider placed in the middle to separate men from women.

Aunt Emma, an accomplished hostess, made arrangements for myself and those spouses who had elected not to convert to Islam when they married into the family. We were invited to sit in adjoining reception area, where amidst giggles a servant gave us a special dessert, which would not be served to the other family members. The pudding proved to be confirmation of the vaunted Indonesian religious tolerance and eclecticism: it was heavily laced with rum.

As the others prayed, I asked my fellow infidels about their respective religions and the problems of inter-faith marriages. I discovered that Indonesia's religious diversity extended into individual families. Increased mobility, especially among the middle class, had led many Indonesians to find life partners far from home towns and native cultures. In most cases, one partner converted to the other's religion, especially if the couple chose to live in a culturally homogenous environment. I remembered Siti telling me of a tourism school classmate who had found a job in Bali. She converted to Hinduism when she married a Balinese co-worker in order to win the respect of her new in-laws, who held all Javanese Muslims in contempt.

Even if one partner did convert, the children might elect to follow their mother's or father's original religion, or would adopt another faith for wholly personal reasons. I was told of one household which included representatives from all religions practiced in the archipelago. They called themselves a Pancasila family, referring to the five guiding principles of the

Indonesian state, which upholds religious freedom and mutual tolerance along with social justice and other noble attributes.

As we discussed religious diversity, the other guests began a rhythmic chanting of *Allahu Akbar*, God is Great. I could see Siti, in her prayer robe, on her knees in the midst of her aunts and cousins, all swaying slightly as the chanting increased in volume and tempo. Whether or not the laced pudding was a contributing factor, I, too, was caught up in the spiritual transport, feeling a sense of community transcending all cultural and social barriers.

After about twenty minutes the chanting subsided, except for several enthusiastic and apparently tireless adolescent boys. Siti and I excused ourselves and proceeded to our next seasonal celebration, a Kemang Christmas party. Though in Kemang any event is an excuse for a party, this and similar gatherings performed an important function that year. The Islamic fundamentalists, flexing their muscles, had lobbied for the closure of all entertainment venues during the holy month. In a typically Indonesian compromise, the city council closed the nightspots and massage parlors, and banned alcohol sales in restaurants during the first two days of Ramadan. Ever resourceful, Kemang expats had stocked up on alcohol and party snacks days before, faxed or e-mailed invitations, and celebrated the Christmas season in time-honored Kemang fashion.

Actually, the party Siti and I attended was quite unlike the raucous bashes of previous years. As many among the expatriate population had avoided the inconvenience of Ramadan and general security concerns by returning to their home countries for the holidays, this was a small and subdued affair, featuring good food and intelligent conversation instead of free-flow beer and general debauchery.

Siti had undergone a remarkable transformation in the taxi. Her baggy pullover had disappeared into her oversize handbag along with her prayer robe, and a few deft tucks, folds, and pins of her blouse, headscarf, and sarong had created a form-fitting outfit capable of turning the most jaded male head. Margarita glass in hand, she held her own in conversations with expat and Indonesian alike. Watching her, I marveled at her ability to slip between dissimilar cultures with the ease of a bird hopping from acacia tree to coconut palm.

Siti's bi-culturalism and the religious diversity of her family were on my mind when I met Pak Trisno the following afternoon, about an hour before sunset. When he offered the customary beer, I declined, citing good manners and respect for another's religious beliefs. I knew the old man was fasting, and I was reluctant to drink in front of him, especially during the final excruciating minutes of a long, hot day without a drop of water. To my surprise, Pak Trisno popped open the cap and placed the bottle in front of me.

"No passage in the Koran forbids the consumption of alcoholic beverages," Pak Trisno said. "Islam only enjoins moderation, sensible advice for believer and infidel alike."

I suspected Pak Trisno's accurate interpretation of Koranic verses was not the only reason for his exceptional hospitality. Pak Trisno often told me of the Javanese mystic exercises he practiced regularly, traditional activities for a gentleman of advanced years. As many of these practices are based on self-denial, perhaps watching me enjoy a cold, refreshing brew while his own parched throat screamed for water was ratcheting his spiritual powers up another notch. At any rate, he would not go overboard: smiling, Pak Trisno advised me not to drink too quickly. In keeping with Islamic precepts of moderation, I would not get another.

As we waited for the sunset call to prayer we discussed the stories of inter-faith marriages I had heard the previous evening. Pak Trisno believes that multiple-faith families are a natural result of the Indonesian attitude to matters of the soul. Though each religion has its fundamentalists, most Indonesians have a relaxed attitude toward religious doctrine, and will happily incorporate diverse influences into their spiritual lives, often dismaying more orthodox co-religionists from other countries. According to Pak Trisno, a Muslim praying with palms at chest level facing upward, a Bali Hindu clasping a hibiscus blossom over her head, or a Christian kneeling with hands pressed together at chin level all reflect a rich mélange of history and tradition, of which the specific practices of their professed religion are only the top-most layer.

The American novelist F. Scott Fitzgerald claimed that the true test of genius is the ability to hold self-contradictory ideas in your head simultaneously without going insane. I am sure Fitzgerald would have dismissed me as a mediocre intellect if he knew the extent to which my reflections on Indonesian religious tolerance were driving me crazy while I was sitting in the gutted shell of the Ketapang Church.

I had responded to an invitation by Stephanie, a client of mine connected with the church, to attend a Christmas Eve liturgy. The setting reminded me of the final scene of a science-fiction movie depicting the survivors of a nuclear or environmental catastrophe worshipping in a ruined cathedral. Rickety auditorium chairs had replaced the vanished rows of teak pews, and a bamboo-and-thatch shelter reminiscent of a nineteenth-century South Sea mission had been erected on the podium, where once had stood a fine mahogany pulpit. Ironically, the congregation themselves seemed out of place. The prosperous, well-dressed worshippers appeared to have nothing more on their minds than praying for the return of good business.

With ethnic tensions in Indonesian still a hot story as 1998 drew to a close, the liturgy had become a big event. A half-hour before the scheduled start, foreign and domestic journalists still outnumbered the congregation. Following the advice of a television cameraman who had previously scouted the building in search of interesting angles, I hopped over a low barrier and climbed the staircase to the balcony, which had been closed for safety reasons. Though the cameraman, in jest, warned me not to make any sudden moves, I knew the concrete balcony, like the rest of the seventy-year-old structure, was perfectly solid. The Dutch had constructed their public buildings to stand for centuries, convinced they would never leave. During the final years of Dutch hegemony the colonialists were condemned as racist oppressors for suggesting that the archipelago's native inhabitants could never build and maintain a stable government and prosperous economy. As I looked around the destroyed interior and recalled the events of the previous six months, I wondered if the arrogant, paternalistic colonialists may not have been right after all.

But from my perch on the empty balcony on this pleasant late afternoon the tensions smoldering throughout Jakarta were another world. Much of the church floor area was open to the sky or covered by sheets of blue construction plastic flapping in the gentle, late-afternoon breeze. Smoke patterns on the bare walls suggested an intentional artistic effect, something you might find in a progressive, non-denominational house of worship in the American Southwest.

I was pleasantly surprised to see Monica emerge on the balcony. She gave me a warm smile and walked to the edge, stepping onto the low concrete riser, the only remnant of the protective handrail. Snapping off pictures without flash in the dim light, she leaned into open space with a photographer's blithe disregard for personal safety. When she finished, she sat beside me and we caught up on news and gossip, as we had not met since working on the rape video. I complimented her on her new close-cropped hairstyle, saying she looked like a war correspondent.

Shortly afterward the service began. The preacher sidestepped the issue of social reconciliation and urged his predominantly Chinese flock to look inward, to accept the horror of the rapes and riots as an unfathomable manifestation of God's overall design. Christians have suffered since the first days of the faith, he said, and Christianity is, at heart, the religion of an oppressed but stalwart people.

"Just as the saints steadfastly held onto their faith through trial and tribulation, we also will survive and prosper."

Alone on the balcony, Monica and I could hold a whispered conversation without disturbing the service. When the preacher told of church members coming up to him and saying, with heartbreaking distress and confusion, "How could they burn down our church? What have we done to them?" I said to Monica: "Besides dominating the economy and treating the pribumi like third-class citizens, nothing I guess."

She replied with a withering look. "Only a few Chinese people are like my 'Uncle' Liem. Most of us try to live good lives and get along with everybody."

But is that enough, she wondered? When the preacher ranted about Philistines at the gates and trials to be endured, Monica told me she need only hop a bus down to her campus to be among friends. While she is unmistakably Chinese, her photography club colleagues and fellow student activists treat her no different from a pribumi.

"There must be something else we can do," Monica said, more to herself than to me. "Maybe all the horrible events this year were not trials to be endured but lessons to be learned."

Monica left immediately after the service to join her family for Christmas Eve services at their own church. To avoid traffic on the congested street in front of the building, I decided to stroll through the kampung behind the church and take a taxi from the major thoroughfare at the southern perimeter of the neighborhood.

If any time is pleasant for walking in Jakarta, it is the hour before sunset during the dry season, which had extended into December that year because of El Niño, yet another tribulation besetting the nation. The sinking sun breaks through the smog, casting a halcyon glow, reflected from the glass commercial building façades onto the whitewashed or pastel concrete walls of kampung dwellings.

Smiling and nodding, responding to the genial greetings I received every few meters, I walked along a tree-shaded path with a canal on my right and a line of tidy dwellings on my left, all doors open to catch the late afternoon breeze. I am always amazed at the amount of furnishings Jakarta's kampung dwellers can shoehorn into their cramped residences. The open doorways revealed tiny living rooms filled with all the amenities of a middle-class home. Most residences contain not only a television and video player, but plush chairs, or a glass cupboard filled with the kitschy European knickknacks beloved by an older generation of Indonesians. Often there is an aquarium, sometimes placed outside for lack of room in the house. This strikes me as a sign of stability, since a fish tank is not easy to pack up and move around at short notice.

I tend to think on my feet, not in the sense that I am particularly quick-witted, but rather that I seem to hold my concentration and think more clearly when in physical motion. Ambulatory musing is highly rewarding in a downtown Jakarta kampung such as Ketapang, inhabited by people from every corner of the archipelago seeking a better life in Jakarta. Every few steps brings a new experience, a giant portrait of Christ on a Manado family's wall; Batak or Ambonese voices singing in harmony.

Eighteen years previously I had received a crash course in the Indonesian ethnic mosaic, while supervising seismic survey crews in the Kalimantan oilfields. The Batak foremen, who were mostly Christians, held the Muslim Bugis making up the labor force in utter contempt. When I mentioned these ethnic tensions to my boss, an old Indonesia hand, he told me not to worry about supposed distinctions between Indonesian tribes.

"I have worked all over Indonesia," he said. "They are all the same."

At the time I regarded his opinions as patent nonsense. Guidebooks and tourist brochures go to great lengths to map the great social, cultural, and linguistic diversity. Almost two decades on, I wonder if that cynical old camp boss was not right after all. A Batak foreman and Bugis laborer will regard each other with mutual disdain, only to band together as fellow "outer islanders" when a Javanese enters the room. When a foreigner joins them, all three immediately become Indonesians, ethnic and religious differences abandoned in favor of a transcendent nationality. Perhaps the divisions are fluid, existing only to serve personal or elite group interests.

In the depths of the kampung I lost sight of my landmark office towers. Asking directions from men sitting at a warung, I decided to accept their invitation to join them as they waited for the dusk call to prayer and the end of their fast. The warung owner was placing a tall glass of sweet tea or thick, black coffee in front of each customer. I requested coffee. When the owner placed the coffee in front of me I was seized with a powerful craving for caffeine, having eaten nothing since breakfast and, much worse, having missed the lunchtime cappuccino that keeps me going when running around town. I reached for the glass, then checked myself and dropped my hand.

During the standard interrogation of my nationality, age, and marital status I divulged my profession. They urged me to write about Indonesia, to tell the world that Indonesians abhor violence. When I tactfully mentioned the recent riots, one of my companions waved his hand in contemptuous dismissal.

"*Orang gila*," he said. Crazy people.

"Indonesians are a peaceful people," another said. All nodded in solemn agreement.

A wavering, tuneless call to prayer from the adjacent mosque interrupted our conversation. As we reached for our drinks, holding the tall glasses daintily by the rims to avoid burning our fingers, I felt the spontaneous camaraderie that arises whenever an outsider shows respect for Indonesian social customs or beliefs. For a moment, I was fully and unconditionally accepted into this tranquil urban village. Sipping my coffee and watching the olive-green water of the canal flow quietly toward the sea, I could almost believe that the previous months of turmoil and savagery had been nothing more than a vivid nightmare.

Epilogue

Pesta Demokrasi

During the months following the Christmas and Idul Fitri holiday season, life in Jakarta returned to, if not normal conditions, then at least a state somewhere this side of bedlam. Despite sporadic bomb blasts in and around the city, the social unrest appeared to have left town, moving to several areas in the eastern region of the archipelago, where long-standing disputes between local residents and migrants erupted into mayhem. To my immense relief, peace returned to the Kemang Palace as my little dysfunctional family worked toward mutual accommodation of their various attitudes and eccentricities. Freed from the inconveniences of city-wide turmoil and the distractions of domestic strife, I, like most Jakartans, applied myself to rebuilding a life shattered by the repeated body blows of the previous year.

Then, about a year after the student demonstrations that had led to the fall of Soeharto, Jakartans hit the streets again. This time, the object was not to bring down a government but to elect a new one. In the previous November, the MPR had set 6 June 1999 as the date for Indonesia's second exercise in genuine representative democracy since the nation's founding. As during the 1955 election campaign, Indonesia took the term "multi-party democracy" to comical extremes, with forty-seven political organizations vying for seats in the newly-empowered parliament.

While sharing the infectious enthusiasm rampant during those heady weeks, I also prepared myself for considerable inconvenience. I knew Jakarta's streets would fill each day with boisterous party supporters, creating traffic gridlock which would force me to walk long distances to avoid wasting hours (and rupiah) in an immobile taxi. I also knew I would have to endure constant taunts from marchers brought in from the countryside, many of whom seldom see foreigners and are unsure how to react upon seeing these outlandish creatures. During previous campaigns, I would deflect curiosity and frequent mild verbal abuse by carrying a set of three T-shirts in my tote bag. When compelled to walk, I would first don either the yellow, green, or red shirt, depending on which party was scheduled to hold rallies that day. When a car or truck filled with party faithful passed, I would point to my shirt and raise my hand in the identifying party salute, eliciting joyful shouts of comradeship and delight.

This year, faced with buying shirts in forty-seven garish patterns, I opted instead for a single shirt printed with the logos of all parties in a vain attempt to please everyone. As it turned out, I had few opportunities to don my multi-party T-shirt, as fears of violence and continued economic uncertainty had curtailed most business activities. Instead of going out, I spent most days holed up in the Kemang Palace watching campaign coverage on television, where shots of colorful rallies and witty voter education announcements counterpointed mind-numbing interviews of novice politicians groping to develop the political skills and media savvy needed to contest modern elections. Golkar, the dominant political organization during the New Order era, was ahead of the pack, with experienced spokesmen and campaign advertisements which would credit a major western party.

I was marveling at the creative and technical proficiency of one Golkar television spot when Adam remarked that the spectacular advertisement, which ended with a helicopter shot of thousands of extras on a mountaintop, resembled the hugely expensive commercials broadcasted by cash-rich *kretek* companies during each Idul Fitri holiday season. I then realized that the Golkar commercial was most likely the work of a good friend, a talented American cinematographer who had led the production team for several such commercials. A long-time resident of Jakarta, he had reluctantly returned to his native California when Krismon devastated the Indonesian advertising industry. Two months before the start of the campaign season, I had been annoyed to learn that he had visited Indonesia without getting in touch with me. I then realized that with a young family and uncertain employment prospects in the United States, he could hardly refuse the extravagant fee offered for the Golkar commercial. Though few would equate Golkar propaganda with, for example, Leni Reifenstahl's cinematic glorifications of the Nazis, nevertheless I suspect he had been too embarrassed to show his face in Jakarta.

While Golkar shoveled out cash to maintain the organization's decades-long domination of Indonesian politics, one party stalwart was facing open mutiny in the ranks, as I discovered one afternoon when I visited Pak Adé to pass the time while waiting for that day's campaign rallies to disperse. During the previous three elections, Pak Adé had been responsible for ensuring that every member of his section voted for Golkar, voluntarily or otherwise. As civil servants were required to vote at their place of work, dissenting votes in the ballot box would reflect poorly on the whole office. Pak Adé needed only remind his subordinates of this and let the overwhelming desire of Indonesians for group cohesion do the rest.

The new election law had destroyed this effective coercion system at a stroke by mandating voting day as a national holiday, enabling civil servants to vote in their own neighborhoods. In Deppen's "vanguard of reform" atmosphere, many lower-level staff did not even bother to exercise their new legal rights of voter secrecy. Pak Adé told me how he had to endure open affirmations of loyalty to competing parties during impromptu rallies held in the corridors.

If civil servant discipline was declining, the Soeharto government's other pillar of support, corruption, was flourishing in the freewheeling political environment. Pak Adé complained that New Order corruption was a drop in the bucket compared to mounting reform-era rapaciousness. He had hoped that the enormous demand for campaign propaganda and voter-education materials would generate badly needed business for his printing company. To his consternation, he had discovered that while the orders were indeed pouring in, he would barely break even on most contracts, as election-commission functionaries wanted a sixty-percent kickback.

Pak Adé lamented the new situation. He had begun his career in the film censorship department during the seventies; when a film was submitted for review, he would make master video copies of the original before passing the print on to the censor board to be sliced up or banned completely. He would then sell the master tapes to video distributors.

"We were organized back then," Pak Adé complained. "If one supplier was the first to copy and distribute a popular new film, the others would hold off making copies for a couple of months. Later on, it would be another's turn. These days it is no better than anarchy."

On election day, Siti awoke with the barely contained excitement of a child on Christmas morning. Not only would she vote for the first time in her life, she would be helping to elect her idol, Megawati Soekarnoputri, to the presidency. The first child of Indonesia's first president to enter politics, Megawati had become a hugely popular symbol of hope and renewal. Siti, and many millions like her, looked to Megawati for Indonesia's salvation. Others were not so sanguine. Though Megawati had demonstrated great courage when she defied the massed forces of military and government during the Soeharto years, many observers, myself included, harbored doubts about her lack of political and managerial experience.

Siti told me I need not worry about Megawati being unequal to the job because "her father is always with her." When I asked how she could be so certain of paternal guidance, she told me her own father had chatted with Soekarno the previous week. Evidently, Soekarno's death in 1970 did not curtail access to the revered founding father.

She insisted that I accompany her to the neighborhood polling station, where I was impressed by the solemnity of the voters as they patiently awaited their turn. I felt none of the carnival-like high spirits of the MPR occupation, the student demonstrations, or even the recent campaign. All entered the curtained polling booths with an air of grave purpose, fully aware that their choice might, for once, contribute to meaningful change.

This being Indonesia, farce was never far away. Heri, one of six hundred thousand Indonesians monitoring polling booths across the archipelago, cast a dummy ballot at one station to demonstrate the process to the assembled voters. The final step was to have his index finger stained with indelible ink, a precaution against multiple voting. To demonstrate the ink would remain on his finger for several days, Heri scrubbed it vigorously with soap and water. To his horror and embarrassment, most of the ink immediately washed away, to the audible delight of the crowd. A few frantic telephone calls later, Heri discovered that batches of an inferior, locally manufactured ink had been distributed to several stations in Jakarta and elsewhere, although testing some weeks before had proved the product ineffective. The correct ink was delivered within an hour, and voting commenced.

When counting started that evening, polling stations became the center of attention in neighborhoods throughout the archipelago. Each vote was counted by displaying the ballot sheet for all to see, then noting the vote in the appropriate column of a whiteboard listing each of the forty-seven parties. I hung around my own neighborhood station for an hour or so, observing crowd reactions. I noticed that whenever a Golkar vote was counted, the onlookers erupted in good-natured jeering, with everyone looking around trying to determine which of their fellow residents was the culprit, presumably by observing his or her abashed expression.

This initial glow of satisfaction waned during subsequent days, then weeks, as results dripped in at a glacial pace, infuriating both journalists faced with implacable deadlines and analysts scrambling to justify their consultancy fees. Like a cartoon depicting a modern factory powered by concealed men straining at pedal-powered generators, retracing the path from the election commission's fully computerized media center would eventually reveal a group of sweating villagers painstakingly tabulating local results with pen and paper under a twenty-five-watt bulb. One e-mail, widely distributed among expatriates, lampooned the counting process as "one, two, three, time for a cigarette; four, five, six, nap time; seven, eight, ten, oops, start over." In fact, election officials from the villages to the national election commission were striving to deliver indisputable tallies, terrified that even the smallest discrepancies might lead to accusations of fraud.

When enough votes had been tabulated to allow meaningful preliminary results, the percentages corresponded with most predictions. Megawati's Indonesian Democratic Party of Struggle (PDI-P) won a clear plurality with over thirty percent. East Java voted almost as a bloc for the National Awakening Party (PKB), founded by Abdurrachman Wahid, a revered Muslim cleric with a long history of combating New Order excesses. Golkar, whose intimidation and reward system had remained fully operational outside of Java, Bali, and Sumatra, accounted for most of the remainder.

Other parties obtained single-digit percentages—most not reaching the two percent of votes nationwide required to remain in existence under the new election law. Several of these parties, called by some the *blok sakit hati*, the sore-losers bloc, challenged the results. The entire process was thrown into disarray as the sore losers hounded government representatives out of an election commission meeting and refused to ratify the final vote tallies.

Pak Trisno and I found the sore losers' antics both amusing and alarming. Pak Trisno told me similar stories of poor sportsmanship during the late fifties, when a freely elected parliament proved wholly incapable of effective government. The nation floundered for years as politicians placed narrow group interests over working toward a consensus. In 1959, President Soekarno stepped out of his figurehead role and assumed executive powers, instituting a system he called "Guided Democracy," which turned parliament into a sort of student government where the principal has the final say. Soeharto adhered to the spirit of "Guided Democracy" when he created the New Order political system of three government-sanctioned parties contesting rigged elections for seats in a rubber-stamp parliament.

"We can expect more petty bickering and partisanship this time around," Pak Trisno said. "We can only pray our politicians will be mature enough to place the national interest above all other considerations. Otherwise we will only be preparing the ground for another dictator."

At any rate, the sore losers' protest did not last long. The traditional Indonesian ways of smoothing over differences of opinion—tireless persuasion and veiled threats—finally brought the disgruntled parties into line, and the Republic of Indonesia's second exercise in genuine democracy ended with an all-round sigh of relief.

One afternoon in late August, a former client phoned me and asked, rather breathlessly, if I could drop by his new office, which was in a converted residence not far from the Kemang Palace. I did so, and discovered he was involved in starting up a travel-industry website. Although most of the tourists trickling into Indonesia were bargain-hunting backpackers, my client and his colleagues had decided on a proactive approach to establish their on-line presence, in anticipation of better times to come. I thought this was an admirable endeavor, so I agreed to help out with writing and editing content for the website during the start-up phase.

On my first day of work, I was pleased to be given a well-written contract with a clear job description, as opposed to the vague, equivocal employment agreements I was accustomed to. However, I was puzzled by one clause in my contract. Besides writing and editing content, they wanted me to *membangun kesatuan*, "to create a sense of unity." I soon realized what this meant. The company was a typical website operation, staffed with a motley assortment of marketing people, graphic designers, journalists, and computer experts. All were young, enthusiastic, talented, and committed. Many were skilled professional communicators; but none of them knew how to listen.

Another pleasant surprise on my first day of work was the discovery I had been assigned a capable assistant. Anna, a recent Trisakti graduate, immediately proved herself invaluable by taking responsibility for production of website content, as I spent more time coordinating activities and identifying conflicts than writing and editing. My favorite ploy was to call a meeting and then lock myself and the participants inside the meeting room, declaring that no one could leave until we reached an agreement. On one occasion, shortly before we launched the website, I made special preparations, knowing we had to resolve some crucial issues on that day in order to meet our scheduled launch date. Participants entered the executive meeting room, which had its own bathroom attached, to discover that I had installed a coffee maker and small refrigerator stocked with food. Knowing how Indonesian meetings tend to drag on, even when participants are in general agreement, I had also piled several sleeping mats in the corner and laid out a set of toothbrushes on the meeting table, each labeled with a participant's name.

One day, Anna presented me with a large card on which was printed the website logo, my name, and a photograph of myself. She had decided—and the management agreed—that I needed a press card to facilitate access to tourism-industry events and government offices. As I signed my name and gave the card back to Anna to be stamped and laminated, I wondered if I would ever have the opportunity to use my new credentials for anything besides getting free coffee at a tourism-industry seminar. The city had been calm since the election, the demonstrations and other dramatic events of the past year at last fading into memory.

As usual, I was mistaken in my belief that life had returned to normal. The following week I stumbled right into a demonstration protesting the Indonesian government's decision to withdraw from East Timor, the result of one of Habibie's numerous well-intentioned, off-hand comments. Earlier in the year, in response to sustained foreign pressure to resolve the East Timor issue, Habibie had declared—to the dismay of the military as well as most Indonesian residents of East Timor—that the nation's annexation of the island had brought nothing but strife and heartbreak.

"If the Timorese want their independence," Habibie announced, "they could have it."

Although the resulting referendum was typically obscure and convoluted—essentially a "no" vote supported independence—the Timorese chose to go their own way by an overwhelming margin. The next day violence engulfed the tiny nation-to-be as pro-Indonesian civilian militias began a violent rampage. When the Indonesian army demonstrated its inability (some said unwillingness) to reestablish order, the United Nations persuaded Habibie to authorize an international peacekeeping mission to East Timor. The arrival of foreign troops on what was still officially Indonesian soil sparked an outbreak of rabid xenophobia in Jakarta.

As I approached the demonstration, bystanders shouted at me to turn back, telling me I might be physically assaulted because I was a white-skinned foreigner. Remembering what had happened to foreigners during the May Riots and student demonstrations, in which we had been treated almost as honored guests, I ignored their sensible advice, and instead reached into my tote bag for my new press credentials, and clipped the large laminated card to my breast pocket.

Seeking a panoramic view of the demonstration, I climbed onto a pedestrian overpass. As I watched the trajectories of tear gas cannsiters being fired from the line of troops about two hundred meters distant, I thought of Monica, who had told me she was taking journalism as well as photography courses and spent most of her free time photographing demonstrations and other public events. I phoned her to ask if she might be nearby. In fact, she was at Trisakti, but had received numerous reports from friends on the scene. She implored me to run for my life. A half hour before, a British news crew had been assaulted at the base of the overpass where I was standing.

Looking down, I saw some white-robed, turbaned figures streaming along the roadway toward the front lines. I removed my press card, bolted down the stairs, and ran to a hotel fifty meters in the opposite direction. As I ran, I heard a distant, sustained volley of rifle fire. Looking over my shoulder, I saw that most of the demonstrators had ceased moving toward the front lines and were now running in my direction. The hotel's entrances were already barricaded, so I vaulted over the low fence behind the chest-high hedge running along the perimeter and landed in a heap on the driveway. As I struggled to my feet, I felt the pain of puncture wounds in my palms, then noticed the string of barbed wire concealed in the vines growing along the top of the fence. I wiped the blood off my hands, examined my wounds, which were minor, then looked up to see a security guard calmly letting in guests through a narrow gap in the far gateway.

For the next several weeks, small anti-foreigner demonstrations continued in the background as the nation prepared for the upcoming MPR general session, during which the recently elected legislators, supplemented by appointed representatives from other society groups, would elect Indonesia's next president. Though most believed, given PDI-P's decisive victory in the general election, that Megawati would soon be moving back into the palace where she had spent much of her childhood, others cautioned her not to call in the decorators just yet. Controlling only thirty-three percent of the seats in the MPR, her party could be easily outvoted and the presidency given to another candidate, or retained by Habibie, who had declared his intention to keep his job.

During the session, opposition to Megawati united around a coalition of Islamic parties, who based their rejection of her candidacy on the belief that Islam prohibits women from becoming rulers. With Megawati's victory in doubt, attention focused on Abdurrachman Wahid, whose powerful charisma had not been diminished by deteriorating eyesight and other health problems.

Siti was aghast, convinced that the man the foreign press described as a "half-blind Muslim cleric" would close down the nightclubs and force all women to wear the *jilbab*. Though Wahid—generally known by the affectionate, respectful name of Gus Dur—was widely acknowledged as a moderate Muslim committed to the separation of mosque and state, Siti believed his blindness, diabetes, and other ailments would inhibit him from controlling the Islamic hardliners who had helped him defeat Megawati. To illustrate her point, Siti did a devastating impression of Gus Dur, eyes shut, face a frenzy of tics, and hands outstretched, waddling across the floor and bumping into a wall.

As the penultimate day of the MPR session dawned, the field had been reduced to three candidates: Megawati, Gus Dur, and Yusril Ihza Mahendra, a noted constitutional law authority who extended his candidacy into the morning to make an obscure procedural point. Habibie had resigned the previous day, delivering a gracious, sincere concession speech that should earn him a footnote in history as post-Soeharto Indonesia's first—perhaps only—good loser.

The voting began shortly after lunch. Although state-of-the-art computerized tallying had been installed a few months previously, the representatives were not comfortable with the devices, so the ballots were cast and counted manually. Actually, the announcement of each vote made the occasion one of high drama. Anna and I sat riveted to the screen, as though watching a foot race. Office activity ground to a halt as Megawati pulled into an early lead. Then Gus Dur caught up to and passed her, staying in the lead until all the votes were counted. Delegates crowded around Gus Dur in congratulation, while the nation watched Megawati fighting back tears.

Siti telephoned me seconds afterward, sputtering with rage. I let her rant in one ear while I listened to the television with the other. Correspondents reporting live from the Hotel Indonesia roundabout reported that Megawati's defeat did not go down well with the thousands of PDI-P supporters who had gathered at the site, expecting to celebrate their leader's triumph. Tension had been high in the area since noon, when a small bomb had exploded in some nearby shrubbery. Minutes after demonstration organizers announced the voting result, the crowd began to stream down Jalan Sudirman toward the MPR.

Hearing reports that both Gus Dur and Megawati planned to address the PDI-P supporters, Anna insisted that I accompany her to the MPR. Besides being legitimate news, this was a moment in Indonesian history she did not want to miss. She talked one of the marketing executives into giving us a lift. Fearful of damage to his new sport utility vehicle, he dropped us off at the Semanggi flyover, where we joined the crowd walking toward the MPR.

We never reached our destination. The riot police had set up a barricade at Taman Ria, the spot where they had been humiliated by student protestors ten months before. Brandishing my press pass, I set out for the front lines, but Anna stopped me, saying she would prefer to watch from the pedestrian overpass two hundred meters back. I wanted to stay with her, thinking I might be safer in the company of an Indonesian, so I agreed and walked back. As we climbed the ramp to the overpass deck, I felt a sense of unease, remembering I had almost been trapped on a similar overpass the month before. When we reach the deck, one youth called out "Bule!" with a menacing tone. I flinched, preparing to retreat, but his companion told him to show some manners.

We looked down to see hundreds of demonstrators perched on a lane-dividing barrier, hammering on the metal rail to generate a driving rhythm. From our vantage point we could see some movement in the mass of demonstrators near the line of security forces. I asked Anna what they were doing. She peered at the mob and said: "As far as I can tell, the *joget*," referring to a popular line dance. I looked again, and saw that they were indeed bopping to the beat being drummed out on the rail. Like most of the mass gatherings during the past sixteen months, the occasion resembled a festival, the participants taking a break from daily cares instead of trying to change the world.

I scanned the troops and the dancing demonstrators, then was puzzled to see the roof of a jeep in my line of sight fly upward. A half second later I felt the breathtaking thump of an explosive percussion on my chest. After a moment of shock, the crowd roared and started fleeing toward our position. Anna wanted to descend to the ground, but I reasoned that no one would chose to climb the steep ramp while in panic-driven flight. I cautioned her to wait with me, and we descended only when the crowd movement had abated. Anna reminded me that my original plan would have put us a few meters from the jeep, which was now sending a pillar of black smoke into the sky. I subsequently learned that at least one foreign journalist had been injured in the blast.

Anna and I agreed that we had seen enough of history in the making for one day. As we walked away from the demonstration area, Anna cautioned me to stay in the middle of the road, away from the low hedgerows lining the sidewalk; the bomb at the Hotel Indonesia roundabout had been secreted in a decorative street-side shrub. When we reached the Semanggi flyover and descended to Jalan Sudirman, all evidence of the disturbances taking place a few hundred meters away disappeared. With all access blocked off, the normally traffic-choked roadways were deserted. We paused in the shade of a tree to collect our thoughts. Anna received a call on her cell phone, then told me that the rupiah was trading at 6900 to the dollar, the highest level since Krismon. I looked at my hands, which were still trembling slightly, and decided that, despite bombs and riots, optimism for this benighted nation's future had carried the day.

We parted there, Anna to a friend's house nearby, me to the Kemang Palace for a cold beer and a futile attempt to alleviate Siti's anger and disappointment. Her mood only improved the following afternoon, when Megawati was granted her consolation prize, the vice-presidency. Even then, Siti insisted on referring to Megawati as "my president," like a loyal subject according full royal deference to a deposed monarch.

During the following days, I telephoned or visited many of my Indonesian friends and acquaintances to hear their opinion of their new government. Both Heri and Yani, who I talked to separately since they were still in marital limbo, were satisfied with their new leadership team. Yani, who still entertained doubts about Megawati's ability, approved of her housewifely focus on basic needs. For example, one of Megawati's top priorities was to guarantee that there would be sufficient supplies of rice to last through the coming fasting month, during which time food consumption actually rises due to the large amounts consumed at fast-breaking gatherings and other communal activities.

Heri was more enthusiastic. His government contacts had informed him that Gus Dur was committed to the development of small and medium businesses. This was very encouraging news, boding well for both his worm farming and his new sideline of offering marketing and management consultancy to small-scale businesses.

During the year since we collaborated on the rape video, Monica had maintained contact with Anwar and other social activists, who facilitated her documentation of the perennially oppressed and marginalized urban poor. Her increasingly jaundiced view of Indonesia's military and ruling elite did not leave much room for confidence in the new administration, but she was happy that the new cabinet included the respected Chinese Indonesian economist Kwik Kian Gie.

Pak Trisno, who had met Gus Dur on several occasions during his furniture-hunting trips to East Java, was also satisfied at the outcome, but foresaw trouble ahead.

"One Javanese mystic tradition seeks to answer three unanswerable questions," Pak Trisno said, with the sly smile that indicated he was joking, but I was expected to pay close attention anyway. "Is there a God, what is the meaning of life, and what is Gus Dur talking about?"

"Gus Dur is undeniably brilliant and possesses great vision," Pak Trisno continued, "but is erratic and inconsistent, and has the unfortunate habit of thinking aloud. If the past is any guide, Gus Dur will take some decisive measures, but will confound most people with vague, controversial, and even contradictory statements. The political elite, who are accustomed to clear distinctions and easy certainties, will not be happy. I suspect that after a few months of dealing with Gus Dur they will probably wish they had elected Megawati."

I did not manage to talk to Pak Adé, but could imagine his dismay the week following Gus Dur's election. The new president had once been a magazine columnist and was a passionate, life-long advocate of free speech. One of his first decrees was to abolish the Department of Information. A few days after that surprise announcement, I was watching the television news with Farid, who liked to visit the Kemang Palace to enjoy a plate of Siti's incomparable *nasi goreng*, fried rice. To our delight, we saw scores of Deppen staffers march to the nearby presidential palace to protest their loss of livelihood, where they were met by bewildered palace security troops.

Farid hooted, and shouted "shoot them all!" at the television screen, presumably echoing the sentiments of browbeaten journalists, cowed editors, and former owners of banned publications. I just smiled. With a plate of *nasi goreng* on my lap and a glass of beer in my hand, I settled back to enjoy the incongruous sight of uniformed civil servants taking to the streets like the scruffy students of the previous year. Indonesia's surreal voyage toward a new society was far from complete.

Acknowledgments

Writing books, like almost any modern endeavor, involves some degree of collaboration. I would like to thank, in no particular order: Tino Saroengallo, for convincing me that my friends' stories were worth telling; Nina Masjhur, for background research I needed to put the stories in context; and Rama Slamet, for refusing to allow my cavalier attitude towards fact verification to compromise the accuracy of this book.

I also would like to thank those who read the book at various stages of completion, including John McGlynn and Janet Boileau, who both managed to be simultaneously loyal friends and merciless critics; and my sister Joann McKinlay, who offered the invaluable perspective of someone who has never lived in Indonesia.

I thank my editor, Jamie James, without whose efforts this book would have been only a pale shadow of what it eventually became, and my publisher, Richard Oh, without whom I would be trudging the streets of Kemang peddling photocopies of my manuscript door-to-door.

Others not directly involved in the production of the book deserve mention for their contributions during the writing process. These include my mother, Kathie Rowsome, for her unflagging e-mail and telephone encouragement, and two long-time friends, Gary Hayes and Byron Black, for occasionally providing support of a more material nature. I also express my heartfelt gratitude to Fitri Ermawati, for maintaining a degree of patience exceptional even for a Javanese.

Finally, I must thank those of my friends who have chosen to remain anonymous, so I could tell their stories unabridged and uncensored on these pages.